C000139634

POETRY

READ, WRITE & PERFORM

Activities and ideas to create sparkling poems!

20 practical poetry workshops

Make all your children poets!

By Paul Cookson

AGES 5–11

Teacher's Book

Designed using Adobe Indesign
Published by Scholastic Ltd
Book End, Range Road, Witney,
Oxfordshire OX29 0YD
www.scholastic.co.uk

Printed by Bell & Bain Ltd, Glasgow
© 2015 Scholastic Ltd
1 2 3 4 5 6 7 8 9   5 6 7 8 9 0 1 2 3 4

British Library Cataloguing-in-Publication Data
A catalogue record for this book is available from the British Library.
ISBN 978-1407-15891-4

Author Paul Cookson

Editorial team Red Door Media, Rachel Morgan

Series designer Neil Salt

Design team Neil Salt and Drew Scott

Illustrator Woody Fox

Cover illustrator Tony de Saulles

Every effort has been made to trace copyright holders for the works reproduced in this book, and the publishers apologise for any inadvertent omissions.

Contents

INTRODUCTION

About the book

The Scholastic Poetry Teacher's Book is a teacher's companion for the Scholastic Poetry anthology series. It provides practical ideas and useful starting points for using poetry in your classroom, focusing on many of the fantastic poems across the ten poetry books. All the workshops in this book are ideas I know to be practical – they are some of my favourite 'lessons'.

A bit about me [Paul Cookson]

I've worked in schools for more than 25 years, leading workshops and encouraging children (and teachers) to write and perform their own poems.

I qualified in 1984 and spent five years as a full-time teacher. In 1989 I went part-time and started working as a poet, visiting schools, libraries, festivals and selected front rooms. Over the next five years this grew, until I was only teaching one day a week. So, I made the decision to become a full-time poet and writer. And I've never looked back.

Having had poems accepted into numerous anthologies, I submitted ideas to publishers and have since edited, written and been part of over 50 collections and anthologies. My poems have been included in hundreds more. Book sales are now over a million.

I've not counted them, but by my rough calculations I've probably visited over 4000 schools in that time and led over 10,000 workshops.

So, here I am – over 26 years later – still visiting schools with a bag of poems and a ukulele. Still enjoying it and still performing some of those poems I started out with. Still using some of those same workshops – it's like teaching my favourite lessons over and over again – because they are great fun AND they always work.

This book has taken me back to some of those workshops and has helped me develop some new favourites as well – I hope you enjoy leading them as much as I have.

Have fun!

Can we teach poetry?

Without doubt, teachers love to read poems to their classes. Without doubt, teachers enjoy reading poems out loud. But also, without doubt, teachers feel less confident about teaching poetry.

Maybe it's because poems are mysterious things, often not adhering to grammatical rules. Why start every line with a capital letter, even halfway through a sentence? Why the lack of punctuation? Why finish a verse halfway through a sentence, leave a line, and then carry on? (This is called enjambment by the way – but knowing what it's called isn't very helpful on its own.)

Maybe it's because the poems many of us studied at school were more serious poems by classical poets (who weren't writing for children).

Whatever the reasons, poetry has a mystique and myth about it. This book aims to demystify poetry with practical, everyday approaches that are simple, straightforward and easy to follow. The only resources you'll need are the poems themselves – links to our Scholastic Poetry anthology series are made throughout the workshops.

Age ranges

While I am not going to set specific age or stage restrictions on the workshops (I believe teachers will see the potential for each workshop with the classes they work with), broadly speaking there will be a progression.

I will begin with those workshops that I have found to be most accessible and successful with Key Stage 1, and work through to cover more technical aspects as we proceed through the book.

However, having said that, all the workshops could be explored and enjoyed by Key Stage 2 classes and there will be aspects of some of the later workshops that will be equally accessible and enjoyable to children in Key Stage 1.

As teachers, you know your classes better than I do. So feel free to use part or all of the ideas and strategies and don't be afraid to adapt them as you go along. The children will often come up with inventive suggestions – go with them and see how they work. Remember, ideas are living and breathing. I am not presenting you with rules for writing poems, but suggestions based on what I've tried over the years.

HINTS AND TIPS

Here are a few pointers to help you when writing and performing poems with your class.

Choose what you like

Everybody's tastes are different and you will choose poems for different occasions and different lessons. But one thing must be clear – choose a poem that you like, and that you think the children will like. If you like it, then the chances are your enthusiasm for it will carry over to the children you are working with.

Be prepared

By this I mean, prepare the children before asking them to write their own poems. Don't be in a rush to get them writing – I know that's difficult, time-wise, in schools, but it's really important that the children enjoy the poem and feel positive about the process before they start 'work'.

Find a voice for your poems

Have fun exploring different ways of performing and bringing a poem to life.

One of my favourite poets, Dr John Cooper Clarke, often says 'if it doesn't sound any good, it's probably because it's not any good'. Poems only come alive when you read them and perform them out loud – so it's up to you to bring them alive and find a voice.

I know from going round schools that teachers love poetry – even if they are not always confident about teaching it. They also love performances. But when it comes to 'performance poetry' they sometimes have a block or lack of confidence. It doesn't have to be like this.

Firstly, I believe that anyone can write poetry. I wouldn't be in the job I'm in if I didn't. There are ways and means to enable children, teachers and parents to write their own poems. And it's easy. Trust me – I'm a poet!

Secondly, I believe that performance poetry is often the best way into poetry for many people. It doesn't rely on lots of text, metaphors, similes and 'poetic words' – it's all about feel and sound.

I think every poem has a voice and when we read and perform poems we bring them to life. It's worth trying different ways of performing a poem until you get the best voice for it. I won't say the 'right' voice, as it need to be what works best for you, and what works best for you may not work for everyone.

Our job is to try to find the best voice to do that. Sometimes that will be the voice of a child, parent, teacher or character in the poem. Sometimes, the style and subject matter will necessitate a certain voice.

One of the great things about performance poetry is its versatility in relation to age groups. Many performance poems work equally well with both Reception and Year 6 – simply because it's not about language and vocabulary, but about sound and feel.

You have to try them out loud. Try taking a look at the poems listed on page 78 and see if you can come up with the best way of performing them. Consider these aspects in your delivery:

- Rhythm
- Beat
- Expression
- Tone of voice
- Loudness or quietness of your voice
- Speed of delivery
- The mood of the poem
- The character(s) in the poem
- Repetition – find a line that you like and repeat it several times

Remember, every word is important. Poets take time over their words when writing them, so it's important to make sure that every word is performed.

Read the poems six or seven times at least with your class and then think about ways of performing. This way, once you are familiar with the lines and layout of the poem, you can concentrate on the feel of the words and how to best perform them, rather than concentrating on just getting the words right.

All poems (with the exception of shape poems and calligrams) benefit from being read aloud and performed. Even 'difficult' or classical poems in old-fashioned language benefit from being performed, helping the rhythms and structures (which are often impeccable) come to life and take on new resonance and meaning.

Get to know the poem with the children through the performance you create. For example:

- You can act as the leader, saying each line for them to repeat, thereby setting the rhythm, mood, tone, speed, and so on.
- Divide the children into groups, giving each group a different line, couplet or verse.
- Have a section that everybody participates in, such as a repeated line or chorus. If there isn't one in the poem already, discuss with your class which lines they would like to repeat and create your own chorus or repeated line.

The main point with performance and poetry is to have a go. Don't be frightened of 'getting it wrong'. There is no such thing as getting it wrong. Only by performing the words out loud will you know how they feel and how they sound. If you do this as a class exercise regularly, the children will get used to it and will start to think in terms of performance. You will both know if something doesn't quite work. They might say 'It doesn't sound right' or 'That line's too long' or 'That word is difficult to say'. You don't have to use the correct terminology, such as 'syllables', to explain and understand what they are talking about. Try saying the lines or words in different ways to see what's best. The important thing is to HAVE FUN!

For a selection of poems that particularly lend themselves to performance, see Poems to be performed in the Appendix, page 78.

Record your ideas

It's worth spending as much time as you can with your class on ideas. Talk about them, discuss them and share them, but make sure you write them all down – on a board, flipchart, or whatever works. Ensure the class can see them and refer to them. Follow up the ideas, if they are good ones, and see where they take you.

Draft and redraft

Once you've recorded your ideas, whether as a group, class or as individuals, you will need time to draft and redraft. No poem is ever finished after the first draft. Poetry is about finding the best words and putting them in the best order. Sometimes that will mean replacing words with better ones (thesaurus at the ready!). Sometimes that will mean taking words out. Sometimes that will mean repeating a line that works particularly well.

Most drafting and redrafting will begin with reading the poem out loud. Explore the sound and the feel of the words. This is often instinctive. Go with what sounds and feels right. Read the drafts out to each other – others may hear things and recognise lines that you don't.

> **"No poem is ever finished after the first draft. Poetry is about finding the best words and putting them in the best order."**

Decide if it needs to rhyme

Most people associate poems with rhymes, which is fine. I love rhymes – a great rhyme is extremely satisfying. However, getting a good rhyme takes time. What usually happens is that children will think of the first rhyme that comes to them and then crowbar this into the poem.

We will look at rhymes and how to get the best ones later, but the only criterion is this: the rhyme must fit the poem. Don't make the poem fit the rhyme. For this reason, I would stay away from rhymes unless they occur naturally.

Consider punctuation and spelling

As poetry tends to bend and break the literacy rules anyway, I wouldn't worry too much about commas and full stops. Exclamation marks and question marks work appropriately. Ellipses are a useful device to denote space and what is to come.

For some reason, most poems begin each line with a capital letter. Unless you'd like to explore the effect of not doing this, you may as well carry this on, using capitals for the things you'd usually use capitals for.

Capitals can also be useful to indicate a loud noise or someone shouting. For example, *BANG!* looks much better than *bang!* and *TURN THAT MUSIC DOWN!* is more effective than *Turn that music down!*

Wherever possible, ensure spelling follows standard rules. However, sometimes the nature of the poem may lend itself to phonetic spelling or exaggerated spelling. For example, *Doowhyafftoooooo?* conveys much more than *Do I have to?* Equally, *TUUUURRRRRNNN IT DOOOOWWWWNN!* gives more sense of the tone than *TURN IT DOWN!*

Also, it's fun not to follow the literacy rules!

Lay out the poem

Once the poem has been drafted and redrafted, there will be a final, neat copy. Often, when children draft a poem, it looks more like a story – a solid block of writing – yet when they read it out, it sounds like a poem. It sounds like a poem because of the pace and the pauses – where they stop, take a breath and so on. This must be reflected in the way it's set out on the page.

I can't remember which poet said it, but I like the definition that poetry is 'that stuff with the white spaces round it', as in the lines don't go to the edge of the page. When setting out a poem, here are a few tips and hints.

Rhyming poems

These are often easier as the lines often end with the rhyme, so there is a natural and more obvious order to follow. For example:

> The bathroom has gone crazy – far beyond belief
> The sink is full of spiders and the toilet seat has teeth

However, this also works:

> The bathroom has gone crazy
> Far beyond belief
> The sink is full of spiders
> And the toilet seat has teeth

It's all about how you say it, where you pause, when you take a breath, and how it feels.

Poems that don't rhyme

This is not as obvious as rhyming verse, but the principles still apply – how you say it, where you pause, when you take a breath, and how it feels. Let's look at an example of a block of writing and see how we can set it out differently:

> My brother really annoys me he comes in my room without asking and reads my diary and then he messes things up and I get the blame and have to tidy it up when it's not my fault

This is typical of how a child might have written it. I often write this on the board and read it with the class to find where the natural gaps are and where the next line begins. So, you could have this:

> My brother really annoys me

Or equally:

> My brother
> really annoys me

Or maybe:

> My brother
> really
> annoys me

Or even:

> My brother
> really annoys
> me

It will depend on how you say it and where it feels natural to take a breath. Often, I encourage the children to go through their own text and mark a line where they will start the next line. For example:

> My brother/ really annoys me / he comes in my room / without asking / and reads my diary / and then he messes things up / and I get the blame / and have to tidy it up / when it's not my fault

This can then be rewritten as:

> My brother
> really annoys me
> he comes in my room
> without asking
> and reads my diary
> and then he messes things up
> and I get the blame
> and have to tidy it up
> when it's not my fault

This works better, but you can then edit it, too. For instance, you can reduce the repetition of *and*. In poetry, we can write in phrases and our brains will automatically put in the extra words, as it's the overall meaning that's important. So, you can then edit it down to this:

> My brother
> really annoys me
> he comes in my room
> without asking
> reads my diary
> messes things up
> I get the blame
> and have to tidy it up
> when it's not my fault

Verses and stanzas

Put simply, you would usually start a new stanza where there is naturally a bigger pause, maybe where the subject changes. Using the example above:

> My brother
> really annoys me
>
> He comes in my room
> without asking
> reads my diary
> messes things up
> I get the blame
> and have to tidy it up
> when it's not my fault

As an experiment, select a few poems from the books and type each out as a continuous block. Then either go through them together with the children, or let them work in pairs, to decide how they should be split up. See how they turn out compared to the originals. As with many things in poetry, there isn't a definitive right or wrong answer.

> "As with many things in poetry, there isn't a definitive right or wrong answer."

Create model poems

Because we will be following guidelines and structures, when the children have finished their poems many of them might look and sound the same. Does this matter? Of course not! We are teaching children the mechanics of how to write a poem, not how to be a poet.

There is an idea that poetry must be individual and somehow uniquely magical – an expression of creativity. And this is what we are looking for, eventually. But in the short term, we want children to feel positive and confident about their poems. We want to teach them how to succeed. If that means all the poems are very similar, so be it.

Say you ask a child *What's two plus two?* and they say *Four.* If you ask a second child and they also say *Four,* you wouldn't then say *Sorry you can't have that answer – it's already been used.* The right answer is the right answer. We are teaching achievement and success. No one has to fail. Everyone can be a poet and everyone can write a poem.

For a selection of poems that can be used as models for the class to copy and replicate in their own style, see Model poems in the Appendix, page 79.

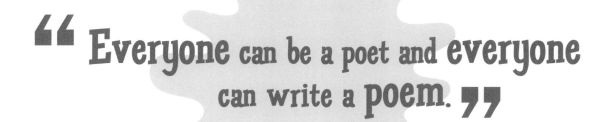

"Everyone can be a poet and everyone can write a poem."

PERFORMANCE POETRY 1

Performance poetry is exactly that – poetry to perform. It's all about how it sounds and the different ways it can be spoken.

Read and perform
'Naughty Uncle Norman' by Stan Cullimore from *Disgusting Poems*, pages 46–47. This is a fun poem about a naughty uncle who is always on the children's side.

Read and perform the poem together, using the notes on page 6 to support you. Focus on the rhythms and the jokes and try to get the best out of these when you perform it. Look particularly at the end of the poem and how to pace it.

Discuss
- Discuss the poem with your class. Which parts did they like most? Which things that Uncle Norman did were the funniest? Make a list of these on the board.
- Were there any words that the children didn't understand (such as *gurning*)?
- Mention the rhymes and the alliteration, and how they add to the feel of the poem.
- What happens at the end of the poem? It's important that the children understand that Naughty Uncle Norman is like a little boy at heart.

  Ideas for your own poems

 Step 1

Imagine Norman as a little boy in school.

Write 'Naughty Norman' on the board.

Step 2

Write a list of all the things Norman might do at school that are naughty. For example:
- things in the classroom
- things to the teacher
- things with other children
- things in the playground, dining hall or corridor
- things with other people's food or work.

This will be lots of fun – you'll get answers such as:
- *He shouts out loud.*
- *He throws his food.*
- *He sticks his tongue out.*
- *He climbs up the walls.*
- *He jumps on the chairs and tables.*
- *He rips up people's work.*

TIP

I usually work with about eight lines to start with.

Step 3

Lead the class by saying the lines out loud for the children to repeat. Set the rhythm, tempo, tone of voice and so on.

Some will work better than others – this is not a problem. Much of the redrafting will be done during the performance rather than the writing, because 'it doesn't sound quite right' or 'it doesn't fit'. You will only find this out when performing it.

Rather than saying *He shouts out loud*, it would be better to preface this with *Naughty Norman*, to help the rhythm. For example:

> Naughty Norman shouts out loud
> Naughty Norman throws his food

These work, especially if you exaggerate the rhythm in *Naugh-tee Nor-man*.

Step 4

Some lines won't work so well, such as *jumps on the tables and chairs* and *rips up people's work*. Rather than reject or rewrite the children's ideas, what I usually do is rearrange them:

> Naugh-tee Nor-man jumps on chairs
> Naugh-tee Norman jumps on tables
> Naugh-tee Norman rips up work

So breaking the lines up or slightly rearranging them will make them work easily.

Then try it again all the way through. After the last line, if you say *What's his name?* the children will almost always shout *NAUGHTY NORMAN!* This then gives you a chorus:

> What's his name? NAUGHTY NORMAN!
> What's his name? NAUGHTY NORMAN!

Divide the class into groups for each verse, so you will have verse, chorus, verse, chorus.

Try it all the way through.

Step 5

Depending on class size and ability, divide the class into groups and invite them to write four lines each. This could be random or, to avoid repetition, give each group a different theme, for example:

- Class
- Playground
- Dinner hall
- Corridor or cloakroom
- Work and displays

Rehearse the lines, maybe say each one twice. Then put it all together in one performance piece. Let everyone say the chorus, then go round each table for the verses (verse, chorus, verse, chorus), all the way through.

TIP

It's likely that you'll have children in some of the groups who are shy, less confident or quiet. If so, organise it so that their verses go in the middle sections, starting and ending with strong groups (you'll know which ones to choose). The overall effect will be strong, as the chorus picks up the rhythm again, if any verses falter, and you start and finish strongly.

Follow-up activities

Create a class

- We've had Naughty Norman, but what about other people in the class? With your class, think of other words that are like naughty, such as *bad*, *loud*, *silly*, *rude* and *horrible*.

- Then think of alliterative names to go with them. For example, *Bad Ben*, *Loud Laura* and *Silly Sarah*.

TIP I tend to stay away from the names of any class members.

- Repeat the process you've already done with Naughty Norman with these and you have a whole class full of naughty children.

- This time, instead of having a chorus of the person's name, just have four lines about each of them and a general chorus, such as:

> We're bad, we're mad
> The worst class in the school!
> We make the teachers sad
> The worst class in the school!

- Alternatively, you can make up your own chorus or link.

Character display

- This makes a great display too. Create 'wanted posters' or 'school photos' of the characters. Invite the children to draw cartoon faces for each of the characters and include the verse about them below.

Keep it positive

- You can do this with positive characteristics as well. Think of favourable words, such as *helpful*, *kind*, *friendly* and so on. Add alliterative names again, such as *Helpful Harry*, *Kind Karen* and so on.

- Using the same process, write a performance piece about the best class in the school.

- A possible chorus could be:

> We're cool, we're ace
> The best class in the school
> The teachers think we're great
> The best class in the school

PERFORMANCE POETRY 2

Read and perform

'My Mother Says I'm Sickening' by Jack Prelutsky from *Family Poems* page 102. This is a humorous and slightly anarchic poem about a boy being told off by his mother for playing with his food.

Read and perform the poem together, using the notes on page 6 to support you. Focus on the rhymes and humour in this poem, which are lots of fun, along with the farcical imagery. There's also plenty of alliteration to get your teeth (or your tongue) into.

Discuss
- The beginning of the poem is lower case while the main section is in capitals. Ask the class why this is. Does it make a difference to the way we say the words?
- Talk to the children about the sorts of things that are said by parents or carers in their homes. Ask: *Are these things said in your house? Which one is most used? Who says them most?*

 ## Ideas for your own poems

 Step 1

Make a list of the phrases that the children suggest. For example:
- *Go to bed.*
- *Tidy up your bedroom.*
- *Turn the TV down.*
- *Clean your teeth.*

 Step 2

Act as the leader, saying the phrases for the children to repeat after you.

Discuss how a parent or carer might say them, focusing on their tone of voice, volume and so on. They don't have to be shouted as loud as possible – doing this loses the rhythm.

> **TIP**
> I usually start by writing eight lines on the board. This is enough for the class to get involved, and later these eight lines can become two four-line verses.

 Step 3

Next, add a chorus, such as:

> Nag nag nag – yap yap yap
> Parents always on your back
> Don't do this – don't do that
> Nag nag nag – yap yap yap

Then divide the lines into four-line verses, separated by the chorus, and you have a poem (chorus, verse 1, chorus, verse 2, chorus).

Divide the class into groups, inviting each group to write their own verse. Four-line verses work well, but see what they come up with.

Step 4

Let each group focus on a different time of day and the particular things that may be said then. For example, in the morning:

> Get up out of bed
> Come and get your breakfast
> Have you cleaned your teeth?
> You're going to be late

Other verses could focus on getting ready for school, coming home from school, tea time and bed time. If you're feeling brave, you can include a verse about what the teachers say.

Ask each group to rehearse performing their verse and then put together as a class piece, with the structure: verse, chorus, verse, chorus and so on.

 # Follow-up activities

Build it up

- Working individually, or in small groups, take one of the phrases and build a whole poem around it.

- Explore a phrase that is said most often, such as *Tidy your room*. Consider who says it, what it means, when it's said, where it's said, how it's said, and so on. Encourage the children to provide the detail or story behind the phrase.

- Tell the children to use a conversational tone, imagining they are speaking to a friend. So they may have something like:

> Mum always says the same phrase
> TIDY YOUR ROOM!
> Every day – every minute of every day
> She always says
> TIDY YOUR ROOM!
> Even when it's not messy, she still says
> TIDY YOUR ROOM!
> Sometimes she shouts
> Sometimes she moans
> Sometimes she gasps
> She always goes on and on and on…
> TIDY YOUR ROOM!

- Note the repeated line *TIDY YOUR ROOM!* helps to give it structure.

- Encourage the children to give details, exaggerating the number of times she says the phrase or the things that are untidy.

- When the children have a first draft of an original piece, invite them to read it to the rest of the class. Ask: *How did it feel when you read it? Were there any parts you really liked? Were there any parts you didn't like?*

- Give them time to add sections or repeat the lines they liked. Let them take out, rewrite or redraft the sections they didn't like. Then invite them to read it out again.

PERFORMANCE POETRY 3

Read and perform

'It Isn't Me – Honest' by Moira Clark from *Family Poems*, pages 78–79. This is an amusing distasteful poem about someone's bad habits around the home – from leaving the loo seat up, to wiping bogies on the wall.

Read and perform the poem together, using the notes on page 6 to support you. The poem doesn't rhyme but has a strong sense of rhythm – most of the lines are short and punchy. Ensure to bring this out when performing it. It's also important to express the child's voice – their feigned innocence and indignation that it could possibly have been them who has done all this (when it is also clear that they have).

There are occasional words that rhyme (*door/floor*, *all/wall*), but it is not a regular rhyming structure. Those rhymes, if exaggerated, may help the performance of the poem. Try it and see.

Discuss

- Introduce the concept that poems don't have to rhyme. This poem has a strong sense of rhythm, which is sometimes more important than the rhyme.
- Talk about the conversational nature of this poem. Point out that the poet's voice is 'normal', that it sounds like someone talking naturally.
- Ask the children which of the things listed in the poem happen in their own homes. Highlight that poems can be about ordinary, everyday things. In many ways, these are the best things to write about as they tap directly into everyone's experiences – the poet's and the reader's. Nothing has to be made up – it can be exaggerated, but it doesn't have to be made up.

 Ideas for your own poems

Step 1

Begin with the following phrase:

> Wozzen'tmeee

TIP
Write the phrase on the board phonetically (you could even have the 'e's going upwards at the end). This will encourage children to consider the performance more effectively than It was not me.

Ask the class to say the phrase out loud so that they understand that it is actually *Wasn't me*.

Invite them to suggest ideas for things they have been blamed or told off for. List these to create the verse. For example:

> Wozzen'tmeee
> Who broke the window
> Who flushed the homework down the toilet
> Who was playing football in the house
> Who ate the last piece of chocolate cake

Step 2

You can now perform this, saying it for the class to repeat. Make sure you use a whingey or whiney voice:

> Wozzen'tmeee who broke the window
> Wozzen'tmeee who flushed the homework down the toilet
> Wozzen'tmeee who was playing football in the house
> Wozzen'tmeee who ate the last piece of chocolate cake

Step 3

As you perform these, you will notice that each line has a different rhythm. This not a problem – it still works. However, if you want to work on rhythms for the poem, you could look at picking out the parts that sound best.

Looking at each line, the first one works fine.

> Wozz/en't/meee/who/broke/the/win/dow

Whereas the second line is long and a bit clunky. You could cut it:

> Wozz/en't/meee/who/flushed/the/home/work

Or you could extend it to two lines:

> Wozz/en't/meee/who/flushed/the/home/work
> Right/down/the/toil/let

Similarly, the third line could be cut:

> Wozz/en't/meee/play/ing/foot/ball

Or extended over two lines:

> Wozz/en't/mee/play/ing/foot/ball
> In/the/house/and/broke/the/vase

And finally, the fourth line can just be simplified:

> Wozz/en't/meee/who/ate/the/choc/late

Then you can add a chorus, such as one of the three examples below:

> Mum! Mum! It wozzen'tmeee
> Dad! Dad! It wozzen'tmeee
> Just wozzen'tmeee – riiight!

> Wozzen'tmeee – it woz 'im
> Wozzen'tmeee – it woz 'er

> Always the same
> Always the same
> I always, always get the blame

As before, divide the class into groups, asking each group to write a four-line verse.

Rehearse the verses and then put them together (verse, chorus, verse, chorus, and so on).

Step 4

Looking back at the original list, consider what happens to the tone and voice if you add a question mark.

> Who broke the window?
> Who flushed the homework down the toilet?
>
> Who was playing football in the house?
> Who ate the last piece of chocolate cake?

Ask the class who they think would be asking these questions. Can they suggest how they would they say them? This will reveal two distinct voices:

> Who broke the window?
>
> **Wozzen'tmeee**
>
> Who flushed the homework down the toilet?
>
> **Wozzen'tmeee**
>
> Who was playing football in the house?
>
> **Wozzen'tmeee**
>
> Who ate the last piece of chocolate cake?
>
> **Wozzen'tmeee**

Try this as a class performance, with half the class as the adult and the other half as the 'innocent' child. There is lots of fun to be had here.

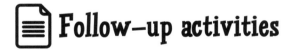 Follow-up activities

Cast the blame
- Try adding *It was...* to blame someone else. For example:

> Wozzen'tmeee who broke the window
> It was my big brother
>
> Wozzen'tmeee who flushed the homework down the toilet
> It was my sister
>
> Wozzen'tmeee playing football in the house
> It was Dad

Start afresh
- Instead of saying *Wozzen'tmeee*, start with *I did not*:

> I did not break the window
> I did not eat the cake
> I did not flush the homework
> I did not play football in the living room
>
> It must have been...
> It can't have been me!

Go crazy

- Invite the children to exaggerate, making up crazy things, such as:

> Wozzen'tmeee who glued the hamster on the ceiling
> Wozzen'tmeee who put the itching powder in Grandad's slippers
> Wozzen'tmeee who beamed my baby brother into outer space with the ray gun I made

Tell a story

- Or encourage them to create the story behind it:

> Wozzen'tmeee who broke the window
> It was my brother
> He was playing football with his friends
> And one of them kicked the ball
> And it went straight into the window with
> K-E-R-A-C-K-I-T-Y-C-R-A-S-S-S-S-H-H-H-H!!!!
> Tinkletinkletinkle
>
> And mum came out and…

- Other phrases that also work well include: *I always get the blame. I'm telling of you!* and *Do I have to?*

- During this workshop, other everyday phrases will also come up that you might think could work. Try them – they probably will!

COUNTING POEMS

Counting rhymes are fun to perform as they have a definite structure and the class can see or predict the numbers.

Read and perform

'Ten Dancing Dinosaurs' by John Foster from *Dinosaur Poems,* pages 64–65. This rhythmical and rhyming poem counts down dinosaurs dancing in different ways. It uses a familiar structure, encouraging the reader or listener to predict the numbers and rhymes.

Read and perform the poem together, using the notes on page 6 to support you. Encourage the children to join in with the number rhymes on the second line of each couplet. They could also count down on their hands as the poem progresses.

Discuss

- Having read the poem together, ask the children which parts they liked best and why.
- Talk about the rhymes, discussing which numbers have the most or least possibilities. Can the children suggest alternative rhymes?
- Point out that this is a counting poem, but it works as a countdown, so we can predict the rhymes. Do the children know any other countdown poems?

 Ideas for your own poems

 Step 1

John Foster used a counting framework for his poem. This countdown is a helpful structure, which you can use for your own class poem.

Invite the children to write a space-based countdown poem (though this works equally with any other subject or theme).

Write the numbers 10–1 vertically down the left-hand side of the board, with *BLAST OFF!* at the bottom. Read each number out together, from top to bottom. Already you have a feel for the poem – it is performable and alive.

 Step 2

Ask the children to imagine what they can see from their rocket-ship window. What can they see ten of in outer space? They may say *ten moons* – this is fine, as it doesn't have to be our galaxy or universe. Let them be as creative as they want. Write it down as such:

> 10 moons

Invite the children to fill in the gaps. Ask: *What colour are the moons?* This will give something like this:

> 10 pink moons
> 9 green aliens

Carry on until you reach *BLAST OFF!*, without repeating any colours or space-based words.

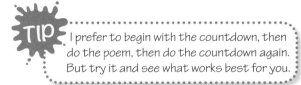

It is likely that you'll end up with lines like *Red rockets* and *Silver stars.* Ask: *Why does this sound good?* If someone gives you the term 'alliteration', feel free to explain it or use it, but don't feel you need to get bogged down by it or that every line has to be alliterative.

Once you have a complete list, try saying it out loud. Say each line for the class to repeat:

> 10 pink moons
> 9 green aliens
> 8 red rockets
> 7 silver stars

TIP I prefer to begin with the countdown, then do the poem, then do the countdown again. But try it and see what works best for you.

Step 3

How can you make the poem better? Firstly, consider if some of the colours and space features might work better in a different order. Try them and decide. Then, add some verbs that end with 'ing'. Ask the class to suggest what each of the objects are doing. For example:

> 10 pink glowing moons
> 9 green wobbling aliens

Perform the poem again. Start with the countdown, then the poem, and then the countdown again. Consider how it sounds. Are there any words that don't sound right or need changing? Can the children think of any better words? Rework it until you are satisfied.

Follow-up activities

Expand the universe
- You can easily make this into a 40-line poem by thinking of three extra words for each space object:

> 10 pink glowing moons
> 10 pink shadowy moons
> 10 pink lumpy moons
> 10 pink full moons

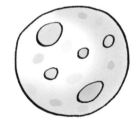

Change the structure
- Alternatively, you could try changing the order of the words around and repeating some.

> 10 pink moons – glowing glowing glowing
> 9 green aliens – wobble wobble wobble

- Or extend the existing lines. Invite the children to suggest what the objects are doing, where they are, when they were doing it, how they were doing it. For example:

> 10 pink moons glowing brightly in the dark

- Challenge them to create similes, such as:

> 10 pink quarter moons
> glowing brightly in the dark
> like smiles of angels

MONSTER OR CREATURE POEMS

Everyone likes monsters and strange creatures – they are fun to create and write about. This workshop is one of my favourite poetry recipes. I say 'recipe' as you will have a list of ingredients, instructions and a few rules to follow, which will give you your first draft.

Read and perform

'It' by Eric Finney in *Spooky Poems*, pages 72–73. This is a mysterious poem about an ominous creature coming up from the sea, only referred to as *It* throughout. We are given clues about what *It* looks like, what *It* does, but we don't actually know what *It* is.

Read and perform the poem together, using the notes on page 6 to support you. Look at the rhythm and rhyme together. Explore if it works better when said slower, savouring the words and images. Or if it's more effective when performed quickly.

Try stressing the *It*. Explore different ways to make the poem sound mysterious when you say it.

Discuss

- Once the class have had a chance to read or listen to the poem a few times, discuss which lines they liked best and why.
- Talk about the repetition of the word *It*. What effect does this create? How would this change if you replaced *It* with *the creature* or *the monster*?
- Ask the children which rhythms and rhymes worked best and why.
- Focus on descriptive words such as *oozed* and *squeezed*. What effect do they create? How should they be said? Are there any other words like these?

 ## Ideas for your own poems

Step 1

Ask a volunteer to think of a number – any number is fine (I usually ask for a number between one and ten). Write it on the board, for example: *seven*.

Then ask: *What has our creature got seven of?* You'll get lots of answers and there are no wrong answers as such.

Inevitably, though, some children may say something like *bottoms* (which is very funny obviously). There's nothing wrong with the word *bottoms* in a poem. However, if you want to move or deflect away from this, you can do this without rejecting their ideas totally. Say: *Well, that's a good idea, but what did everyone do when you said the word 'bottoms'?* (Everyone laughed.) Ask: *If everyone laughed, do you think it sounds like a scary or spooky creature?*

Explain that poetry is about choosing **the best words for the poem**. In this case it's scary words. Suggest that if they want, they could look at different types of creatures later, choosing funny, cute or disgusting words, as appropriate.

Write down the answer like this (leaving a gap):

Seven   eyes

Step 2

Next, consider the colour of the creature's eyes. Remind the children about choosing the best words for the poem – pink may be a favourite colour, but does it sound scary?

Seven   red   eyes

Invite the children to think about what the eyes are like. Can they describe them?

Seven   red   fiery   eyes

This then gives you the recipe:

NUMBER	COLOUR	DESCRIPTION	FEATURE
Seven	red	fiery	eyes

Say it out loud first, for the children to repeat after you. Think about your tone of voice, volume and speed of delivery – all of which affect the mood created.

Step 3

It's time to add some verbs ending with 'ing'. Invite the children to think of four words that describe what the monster's eyes are doing, such as *staring*, *looking*, *glowing* and *glaring*. So, you then have:

> Three red fiery eyes
> Staring, looking, glowing, glaring

Try saying it in a rhythm:

> Three – red – fiery – eyes
> Staring – looking – glowing – glaring

TIP

I usually find that four sets of two lines works very well.

Repeat the process with different numbers, colours, descriptions, features and descriptions of what they are doing. There's only one rule – they cannot repeat any of the words.

Step 4

When you have a selection of lines, look at the ideas and pick out the best ones, think of better words, and try changing the order of the words. For instance, in the example above *staring* and *glaring* both rhyme. So you could try:

> Looking, staring, glowing, glaring

There is also alliteration with the 'gl' in *glowing* and *glaring*. You might want to try and make the whole line alliterative. Play about with it and see what happens.

Remember, you don't need to have alliteration or rhymes at all – so don't go looking for them unnecessarily. Go with the best ideas. However, inevitably, you will find alliteration and rhymes or half rhymes, so if they're there already, explore them and use them.

Keep performing the words. You might find that some words don't fit as well as others. Words with two syllables often work best, but it's not a hard and fast rule that words with three syllables don't fit. Some of them do – it depends on how they sound. For example, *shimmering* can be said as *shimm-ring*.

Retreating and words with harsh consonants together are always difficult to say in the context of the rhythm of the poem. Again, go with the feel of the words and what sounds best.

TIP

There is a difference between performing a poem as a group and performing as a single voice. As a group, the rhythm or beat needs to be clear and precise – whereas an individual voice can create their own rhythm, mood, tone and speed.

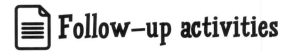

📄 Follow-up activities

Extend the descriptions
● Extend the children's work by taking each verb ending in 'ing' and expanding the sentence. So you could have:

> Seven red fiery eyes
> Staring from its bony skull
>
> Seven red fiery eyes
> Looking left and looking right
>
> Seven red fiery eyes
> Glowing in the midnight gloom
>
> Seven red fiery eyes
> Glaring, waiting for its prey

Create more monsters
● Try writing poems for different types of monsters – scary, cute, funny and disgusting. Explore which words work best for each particular type.
  ● Cute monster: *Four pink fluffy ears*
  ● Disgusting monster: *Four green slimy nostrils*
  ● Funny monster: *Four blue hairy bottoms*

KENNINGS

Kennings are thought to originate from the Anglo Saxons and Vikings, who gave names to their swords. Not names like Fred or Susan of course, but exotic and brave names such as Death Bringer, Skull Smasher, Blood Gusher and Heart Piercer.

So, a kenning is a way of describing something without actually using its name. For example, you could have *tail wagger*, *loud barker* or *stick fetcher* to describe a dog. Or *furniture scratcher*, *mouse chaser* or *loud purrer* for a cat.

Along these lines, you could do the same for footballers, animals, fish, birds, people and so on.

Read and perform
'My Aunt' by Coral Rumble from *Family Poems*, page 43. This heart-warming poem lists the attributes of the poet's aunt, painting a vivid picture using only kennings.

Read and perform the poem together, using the notes on page 6 to support you. Concentrate on the short rhythmic nature of the lines. Try leading the class by reading each line for the class to repeat after you. Can the children suggest actions to do while performing the poem?

Discuss
- Talk about which lines are the children's favourites and why.
- Ask the class to think about their own aunts. Do any of the lines in the poem suit their own aunt? Can they choose one that sums her up best?
- Can they suggest any similar descriptions to describe their aunt that Coral hasn't already used?

 ## Ideas for your own poems

 Step 1

You could do a general, all-purpose football kenning or you could look at a particular role.

Start by looking at a goalkeeper and invite the children to think of all the different things a goalkeeper has to do. Create a list, such as:
- Ball catcher
- Shot stopper
- Ball saver
- Cross snatcher
- Loud shouter

 Step 2

Looking through the list, you might find that you have some repetition, such as *ball catcher* and *ball saver*. If so, look at using alternative words, such as *ball catcher* and *penalty saver*.

You might also find that some of them rhyme, like *ball catcher* and *cross snatcher*. Arrange them in groups of four, placing those that rhyme in lines two and four. For example:

> Shot stopper
> Ball catcher
> Penalty saver
> Cross snatcher

Step 3

Next, take a look to see if there are any other words that could rhyme or half rhyme.

- Stopper/blocker/shocker
- Slider/diver
- Kicker/flicker

Put these together in groups of four, as in Step 2, and see how many verses you can make.

Try to perform these so that the rhythm is pronounced and exaggerated.

Step 4

Divide the class into groups, giving each group a different player to write about:

- Goalkeeper
- Defender
- Midfielder
- Attacker
- Manager
- Referee
- Crowd

By the end of the workshop, you will have created a complete football match experience!

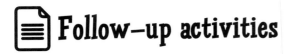 Follow-up activities

Poetry cards

- Kennings can be written about anything. They're great for Mother's Day and Father's Day. When you make cards in class, encourage children to write a four- or eight-line kenning about their mum or dad to make it really personal.

Animal riddles

- Animals are also great subjects for kennings. Give each child or pair a different animal and ask them to write at least four lines about it. Then read them out to the rest of the class. If they have described them well, then everyone should guess them. The aim is not to trick them so they get it wrong, but to describe the creature so that everyone gets it right.

- Talk about the order and best way of using all the ideas. For instance, if you are describing an elephant, then you may get ideas such as:

- Trunk swinger
- Grass eater
- Water squirter
- Heavy mover
- Ear flapper

- Obviously *trunk swinger* is the most obvious and will make sure everyone thinks of an elephant. So to retain the suspense and interest, rearrange the order, bringing the less obvious ones to the beginning, moving gradually through to the more obvious ones at the end. In this way, all the ideas will be listened to:

- Grass eater (any creature can eat grass)
- Ear flapper (many creatures can flap their ears)
- Heavy mover (could be any large creature)
- Water squirter (not all animals squirt water so an elephant comes to mind now)
- Trunk swinger (only an elephant has a trunk, so the answer is revealed)

- Remember, the secret of poetry is putting **the best words in the best order**.

CRAZY CREATURES

In this workshop we are going to look at animals and verbs – don't worry though, this isn't a grammar lesson! Verbs are a simple starting point and, in this case, also work well rhythmically.

The instructions below focus on creepy crawlies, but the workshop can be done just as easily with fish, birds, farm animals and jungle creatures.

Read and perform

'Spider on the Toilet' by Andrew Collett from *Animal Poems*, page 88. This is a short, funny poem about Mum not being able to use the toilet because there's a spider on it. It will make the children smile, mainly because it has the words *spider* and *toilet* in it! I like it because it doesn't over-explain the joke or go into detail about what might happen if Mum sat on the toilet when the spider was there – that's all left to the imagination.

Read and perform the poem together, using the notes on page 6 to support you. Try reading it fast and then slow. Explore the difference it makes. Which words work better when stressed?

Discuss

* Talk about what other creatures the children wouldn't want to find on or near the toilet.
* Ask the class to suggest other creatures that could be found in different parts of the bathroom.

 Ideas for your own poems

 Step 1

Ask the children to think of a range of different creepy crawlies and write them on the board. For example:

* Spiders
* Beetles
* Ants
* Flies

* Butterflies
* Ladybirds
* Snails
* Slugs

 **TIP** Even numbers of creatures work well when performed.

 Step 2

Perform this list as if it were a poem, saying it out loud for the class to repeat. It works best in twos – exaggerate the rhythms in each pair, adding the word *and* to help the rhythm:

> Spi–ders – bee–tles
> Ants – and – flies
> La–dy–birds – and – butter–flies
> Slugs – and – snails

Slugs and snails sound good together because they are alliterative. Some ideas will be naturally alliterative, so there's no need to search out further alliteration.

The rhythms here sound great. You can spend a while playing about with them, repeating each line four to eight times, overlaying the next line over the top like a musical round.

Step 3

Next, add a simple chorus, such as:

> Creepies here
> Crawlies there
> Creepy crawlies everywhere

Then break the original list into verses and add the chorus:

> Creepies here
> Crawlies there
> Creepy crawlies everywhere
>
> Spiders – beetles
> Ants and flies
> Ladybirds and butterflies
> Slugs and snails
>
> Creepies here
> Crawlies there
> Creepy crawlies everywhere

Step 4

Challenge the children to make the poem more interesting by adding some verbs ending in 'ing'. Ask them to suggest what each of the creatures are doing. Ask questions like: *How is the spider moving? What are ants' habits? What noise do flies make?* Add these to your verse:

> Spiders climbing
> Beetles crawling
> Ants carrying
> Flies flying

 TIP Only use each word once. So even though butterflies and flies both fly, encourage the class to think of different words to describe this for each one.

When describing slugs and snails, you are bound to get *sliding*, *sliming* and *slipping* (without even mentioning alliteration) as the ideas lend themselves well to these words.

Perform the whole verse again, with the descriptive verbs and the chorus, emphasising the rhythms.

Step 5

At this stage, you can evolve this into a funny poem. Ask a child what their favourite food is. They often say chocolate or chips or similar – so work this in:

> Spiders climbing on my chips

It works well if you let the children suggest a different food for every line.

Alternatively, think of different places the creepy crawlies could be – in clothes, on parts of the body, in different rooms at home or school, and so on. This will give you something like:

> Spiders climbing on my chips
> Beetles crawling in my socks
> Ants carrying up my nose
> Flies flying in the toilet

Split the class into groups and give each group a different set of insects and different places. Let them work on their verse, rehearsing and performing it, with everyone doing the chorus.

📄 Follow-up activities

Describing bugs

● Rather than (or after) making a funny poem, try creating a descriptive poem. After Step 4, try adding some adverbs ending in 'ly' instead.

> Spiders climbing carefully
> Beetles crawling quickly

● Add colours and description:

> Black spiders climbing carefully
> Shiny beetles crawling quickly

● Add more description:

> Hairy black spiders climbing carefully
> Shiny fierce beetles crawling quickly

● Let the children decide where are they climbing or crawling to, and why:

> Hairy black spiders climbing carefully
> Up the wall to spin a web
>
> Shiny fierce beetles crawling quickly
> Across the garden ready to fight each other

8

BROTHERS, SISTERS AND OTHER ANNOYING CREATURES

It's always good to write what the children already know about. Many will have brothers and sisters of their own, most will have experienced other people's brothers and sisters, and all will be able to imagine having an annoying brother or sister.

Read and perform

'My Little Sister' by Brian Moses from *Family Poems*, page 58. This warm but amusing poem is about a boy who's alarmed by his little sister, who just wants to kiss him. It includes a mixture of lines that rhyme and lines that don't, which give a change of pace and focus. Children will enjoy the 'yuck' factor and the naughtiness of the word *snog*.

Read and perform the poem together, using the notes on page 6 to support you. Try to savour every word (as you should do in all poems), bringing out the rhythm and stressing certain words such as *kick* and *thump*. Try reading it slower as you get towards the end of the poem so that the disgusting nature of the last verse gets maximum effect.

Discuss

● Ask the children why some parts that rhyme work well.
● Can they suggest why it is effective when they don't rhyme?
● Discuss the best way of exaggerating the comical feel at the end of the poem.

 ## Ideas for your own poems

 Step 1

Ask the children to think about their own family. Do they have a sister or brother like that? Do they have annoying habits? List these on the board. You'll get ideas such as:
● They embarrass me in front of friends
● Come in my room without asking
● Always turn the TV over while I'm watching it
● Hit me
● Steal my stuff
● Take ages in the bathroom

 Step 2

Add a phrase at the beginning and end, for balance and emphasis, to turn this into a poem:

> My brother/sister annoys me
> They embarrass me in front of friends
> Come in my room without asking
> Always turn the TV over while I'm watching it
> Hit me
> Steal my stuff
> Take ages in the bathroom
> Yes – my brother/sister really annoys me!

Step 3

You can now break the text into verses and add a *really* to emphasise the frustration:

> My brother really annoys me
> He hits me
> Comes in my room without asking

Miss another line and add a further *really* so that the reader or listener can feel the frustration building up.

> My brother really, really annoys me
> Steals my stuff
> Takes ages in the bathroom

As a class, think about the order of the list. Make sure the actions start from the least annoying and end with the most annoying. This will help aid the performance, too.

Tell your class to imagine their brother or sister is right there, and they are talking about them while annoyed. This will enable them to find the right voice – especially if they are *really, really, really annoyed*.

Step 4

Challenge the children to think of other words or phrases that mean 'annoy me'. For example:

- Bug me
- Get on my nerves
- Do my head in
- Pain in the neck
- Drive me up the wall
- Irritating

Instead of repeating *My brother annoys me*, start each verse with a one of these phrases.

> My brother really is so irritating
>
> My brother really, really bugs me
>
> My brother really, really, really does my head in

Play around with the order of the habits, working with the children to build up to the most annoying for the last verse. Try putting some or all of the phrases together for the end of the poem.

> Yes, my brother really, really annoys me
> does my head in
> gets on my nerves
> bugs me
> And drives me up the wall
> At the same time!
> Soooo irritating!

📄 Follow-up activities

Creating a story

- Expand the poem, so each line becomes a story – a separate poem in itself.

- Working in groups, give each group a line to work on. Encourage the children to think about the scenario, adding as much detail as possible, exaggerating the details, and repeating any phrases they think sound good.

- After they've created a first draft, ask them to read it out and see how it sounds. Encourage them to work on it again, deciding which parts sound good and taking out anything that doesn't feel right. For example, a first draft might be:

> My sister really annoys me
> She spends ages in the bathroom
> Getting ready and doing her hair
> I ask her to hurry up and she just ignores me
> So I'm always late
> Because she spends ages in the bathroom

- Their second draft might add further detail, such as:

> My sister really annoys me
> She gets on my nerves
> She drives me up the wall
> Especially when she's in the bathroom
>
> She spends ages in there
> Ages and ages and ages and ages
> Doing her hair and make-up
> For hours and hours and hours and hours
>
> I ask her to hurry up and bang on the door
> But she ignores me
> Again and again and again
> While brushing her hair
> Again and again and again and again
> For hours and hours and hours and hours and hours
> And it still never looks right
>
> And I'm waiting
> For hours and hours and hours
> Just because she spends ages in the bathroom
>
> Sisters!
> Who needs them?
> They're a pain in the neck!

9 SUPERSONIC EARS

This workshop considers the various sounds that can be heard in school, how these can be turned into lines of verse, performed in different ways and grouped together for effect.

Read and perform
'Do You Know My Teacher?' by John Rice from *School Poems*, pages 78–79. This comical poem is set out as a multiple-choice quiz, describing the poet's teacher. It plays with rhyme and pattern and uses unusual visual imagery to create humour.

Read and perform the poem together, using the notes on page 6 to support you. Try reading it out slowly to exaggerate the possible rhyme – then say all the alternatives. Let the class decide which they think works best, then say it again, one line at a time for the class to repeat

Discuss
- Talk to the children about the humour. Which lines do the children think are the funniest and why?
- Discuss the forced rhyme of *beef* and *teef*? Does that help the humour?
- Ask the children whether they think the repetitive nature of the poem helps the reader's understanding of the poem.

 Ideas for your own poems

Step 1

This can be a fairly straightforward poem to model – create a fictitious teacher and come up with some obvious rhyming words (see Workshop 13, page 47, for more on finding rhymes).

So to extend this idea further, ask the children to imagine a teacher who can hear all the noises in the school – loud noises, quiet noises, near and far noises. In fact, he or she has SUPERSONIC EARS!

Ask the class to suggest all the noises the teacher might hear. Make a list on the board. For example:
- Children talking
- Teachers slurping tea
- Teachers crunching biscuits
- Slamming of the door
- Footsteps banging

After they've given you a few ideas, encourage them to stop, be very quiet and listen carefully for the quiet school sounds. List these on the board:
- The clock ticking
- Pages rustling
- The scratching of the pencils

Step 2

Read out the list as a performance. Encourage the children to think about their voice, their volume, and their tone. Suggest that maybe each line might lend itself to a different voice. Try the lines with different effects:

> Pages rustling
> Slamming of the door
> The clock ticking
> Teachers shouting

Then add a chorus. This is one I usually use, which works well (using either *he* or *she*):

> Supersonic ears
> Everything she hears
> Everything she hears
> With her supersonic ears

Allowing four lines for each verse, the chorus can then be interleaved with the verses in the pattern: verse, chorus, verse, chorus.

Step 3

Once you have performed the poem together, ask the children what they've noticed. Ask: *Do any lines sound particularly good? Are there any that don't sound quite right or that don't fit? Do any sound better when they're together?* For example:

- it may sound better to say *The ticking of the clock* rather than *The clock ticking*
- *The rustling of paper* might be preferable to *The rustling of pages*

Look for any onomatopoeia in the lines and vocalise the sound effect. For instance, the 'ustling' sound in *rustling* could be exaggerated for better effect.

Try grouping the sounds, so maybe all the loud ones are together and all the quiet ones are together, or group all the kitchen noises and all the staffroom noises. Create a rhythm with the structure.

Step 4

As you gather ideas, you'll probably find rhymes, such as *Slamming of the door* and *Footsteps banging on the floor*. Use these as lines two and four in a four-line verse, as they can be spread out and you can slot non-rhyming lines in between. For example:

> The ticking of the clock
> The slamming of the door
> The teachers slurping tea
> Footsteps banging on the floor

This can then be made better by dropping *The* from line three and *banging* from line four:

> The ticking of the clock
> The slamming of the door
> Teachers slurping tea
> Footsteps on the floor

Step 5

If you have any natural onomatopoeia, emphasise this by adding sounds, such as:

> The squeaking of the pens – squeak squeak squeak
> The ticking of the clock – tick tock tick tock

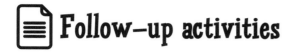 Follow-up activities

Tick tock clock

- Focus on one or two of the sounds and noises and construct a poem around them. For example, the *tick tock* of the clock is a good starting point.

- Look at time and what happens in class as time ticks by:

> Tick tock of the clock
> Children reading
> Tick tock of the clock
> Teachers marking
> Tick tick – tock tock tock
> Tick tock tick tock tick tock clock

- Play about with the sounds and rhythms and see where they take you.

Metaphors and similes

- Extend the ideas by looking at metaphors and similes. For example:

> Slurping tea like horses at the water trough
> The footsteps are a drumbeat of doom in the corridor

Telling the whole story

- Tell the story behind one of the sounds – take one idea and use it as the basis for a whole poem. For example, for the footsteps in the corridor, consider:
  - Are they loud or quiet?
  - Whose footsteps are they? Teachers or children?
  - Are they running or walking?
  - Are they getting closer or fading?
  - Whose footsteps are recognisable? Perhaps a certain teacher has certain shoes?

10

WHEN THE TEACHER ISN'T THERE

In this workshop, you will write a performance poem, using lists, repeated lines and a chorus.

Read and perform

'At The End of School Assembly' by Simon Pitt from *School Poems*, page 19. This list-based poem describes the way all the different classes leave their classrooms. It features puns and wordplay and is lots of fun. The children will enjoy the jokes and exploring the play on words. It's a great starting point for children to model their own poem on. However, we are going to use it as a stepping stone to one of my favourite workshops.

Read and perform the poem together, using the notes on page 6 to support you. Try performing the poem using different voices for different lines. Ask the class whether this adds to or distracts from the poem?

Explore a change of pace. Do some lines sound better slower or faster?

Ask the class how they might say the last line.

Discuss

- Draw the children's attention to the puns and plays on words:
  - Sparrow – flew
  - Steed – galloped
  - Bull – herded
  - Bumble – buzzed
- Which ones do the children prefer? Can they explain why? Ask them to suggest some more if they can. (This could lend itself to a new poem of puns. If the children are inspired by this, then run with this idea while the ideas flow.)

 ## Ideas for your own poems

Step 1

Ask the children to imagine the classroom when the teacher isn't there. What sorts of things might they do? The children will probably have lots of ideas – write their suggestions on the board. For example:
- Have a party
- Rip up the test papers
- Eat our sweets
- Text on mobile phones
- Dance on the tables
- Stand on the chairs

Once you have a list, there are a few ways to turn it into a poem. Try the simple numbered list:

> Ten Things That Happen When The Teacher Isn't There
> 1. Stand on the chairs
> 2. Rip up our test papers and throw them out of the window
> 3. Throw paper planes across the room…

Each of the ideas can be extended, adding detail and colour. Alternatively, use people's names instead of numbers:

> John puts a whoopee cushion on the teacher's chair
> Tracey rips up the test papers
> Nathan sings out of tune while standing on the table…

Try creating a performance poem by repeating the starting line every four lines:

> have a party
> rip up the test papers
> eat our sweets
> when the teacher isn't there
>
> text on mobile phones
> dance on the tables
> stand on the chairs
> when the teacher isn't there

Add a chorus to create a structure and rhythm:

> We don't mind
> We don't care
> When the teacher isn't there (repeat x2)

Then perform it around the class (verse, chorus, verse, chorus). Change parts to make the lines easier to say. For example, simplifying *test papers* and *mobile phones*:

> Rip up the tests
> Text on our phones

Focus on the language to create a rhyming poem. However, beware – children often say *I want it to rhyme* and then think of the first rhyme they can and crowbar it in – even if it doesn't make sense. Remember, the rhyme must fit the poem, not the other way around. The rhyme must make sense.

Start by looking rhymes that occur naturally, with the children. You may need to change them around a little so they sound better. For example:

> stand on the tables
> dance on the chairs
> text on our phones
> when the teacher isn't there

Then move on to look for additional rhymes. Remember, don't put a word in the poem just because it rhymes – it must make sense in the poem. The children may come up with ideas like these:

- hair
- care
- underwear
- beware
- air

Use these in new lines, taking on board the rhythm of the lines:

> boys gel their hair
> paper planes through the air
> girls play football everywhere

Then look at how they will fit together. If you have a four-line verse and the fourth line is *when the teacher isn't there*, then you only need a rhyme for line two. Lines one and three don't have to rhyme. So you can have:

> stand on the tables
> paper planes through the air
> text on our phones
> when the teacher isn't there
>
> put a whoopee cushion
> on the teacher's chair
> this is what we do
> when the teacher isn't there

The children will soon get a feel for the process and the poem will quickly build up.

📄 Follow-up activities

Story-time

● Each of the phrases could become a poem of its own. You could tell the story behind the phrase. For example:

> Miss went out of the classroom
> John got out his whoopee cushion
> Tracey was look out
> John crept forward and placed the cushion on the teacher's chair...

MAKING IT FUNNY

Children love to write poems that make them laugh. In this workshop we will explore various ways to write a funny poem, as well as looking at the use of rhythm, rhyme and alliteration.

Read and perform

'Ernie – the Great Collector' by Patricia Leighton from *Pet Poems*, page 114. Poems about pets in strange places are always funny and this poem works particularly well. The rhythm is great, the rhymes and references are funny and are sure to appeal to children of all ages.

Read and perform the poem together, using the notes on page 6 to support you. This poem has a fantastic mixture of rhymes and alliteration. Exaggerate the alliteration to bring attention to it.

Discuss

● Ask the class which lines they enjoyed most. Can they explain why? Which did they think were the funniest? (The *lizard licking limescale from the loo* will no doubt prove popular!)

● Talk about the last line: *an alligator in the bed*. Point out that it's a strange place for a pet, which will prepare the class well for the workshop.

  ## Ideas for your own poems

Step 1

Ask the children to call out some different pets, and make a list on the board. For example:

● Cat   ● Hamster
● Dog   ● Turtle
● Snake   ● Parrot

You might want to start with the children's own pets, but move on to include exotic and unusual pets, too.

Step 2

You can perform this as a poem by reading the list out loud:

> Cat and dog
> Snake and hamster

Or you could make it a bit more interesting than that, by giving the class a title to guide their ideas. I have a poem called 'When the Wasp Flew up My Brother's Shorts', which immediately suggests something funny without seeing the actual poem. A title can present an image and set a tone, from which you can build.

Tell the class the title is going to be 'That's No Place to Put a Pet'. The rhythm and alliteration in this line work particularly well. Try saying it at different speeds and with different emphasis on the rhythm. Discuss which works best.

Invite the children to think of silly, strange, weird or wonderful places that you shouldn't put a pet. Explain that it's an exaggerated and funny poem, so anything can happen!

Begin each line with *Don't put...* to give you a starting point and an easy structure.

Step 3

Start by looking at rhymes. As we've already noted, rhymes are great but they must fit the poem. Look for the best idea, not necessarily the first. The first idea might get you going though. Ideas are like dominoes – one leads to another and another and then another.

Ask the children: *What rhymes with cat?* There are plenty of rhymes, such as *bat* and *mat*. But not all make sense:

> Don't put the cat on the mat
> Don't put the cat on the bat

However, some will have possibilities:

> Don't put the cat in the hat

Ask the class whose hat would be funniest – Mum's, Dad's, brother's, sister's, Grandad's, Grandma's? I've found they often say *Grandma's*. So you now have:

> Don't put the cat in Grandma's hat

Rhythmically this works and rhymes, too.

Step 4

Not every animal rhymes though, and not all rhymes are good enough. *Dog* rhymes with *bog*, *log* and *frog. Don't put the dog on the bog / log / frog* is okay, but it could be better. So let's consider how alliteration can help.

Ask the children to think of somewhere in or around the house beginning with 'd'. For example:

- Ditch
- Doorway
- Dryer
- Dishwasher

Try them out and decide which one sounds best:

> Don't put the dog in the ditch
> Don't put the dog in the doorway

In my experience *dishwasher* has always been the most popular:

> Don't put the dog in the dishwasher

It has a great ring and feel about it.

Step 5

Finally, look at the possibilities of using silly or random places, such as the *freezer*, *Dad's bath*, *sister's socks* or *Mum's drawer*. For example:

> Don't put the hamster in Dad's socks

It's almost impossible for lines not to work on this basis. The important thing is the rhythm. Keep saying them out loud – if they are not easy to say, edit them until they are.

With all these methods, it's about finding the best lines. Do this as a class exercise, trying out a variety of ideas for each line, until you get a feel for which one works best. There will be a consensus of opinion for the best or funniest – ask the children to vote for their favourite.

Step 6

It's time to put the poem together. Include a repeating line for structure and balance. I prefer it as the fourth line of the verse, as in:

> Don't put the cat in Grandma's hat
> Don't put the dog in the dishwasher
> Don't put the hamster in dad's socks
> That's no place to put a pet!

You don't need to have a rhyme, alliteration and a silly place in every verse. It could be three rhymes, or two alliterations and one silly place – it doesn't matter. It's the rhythm that's important.

Step 7

Make up a chorus, or try this one I often use:

> Hey hey hey! Call the RSPCA
> Hey hey hey! Call the RSPCA
> Hey hey hey! Call the RSPCA
> That's no place to put a pet

This lends itself well to actions, such as:

- Pointing while you say *Hey hey hey*.
- Making a telephone sign with your hand for *Call the RSPCA*.

Perform it as a class, all the way through (verse, chorus, verse, chorus). Either lead the class, saying each line for the class to repeat, with everyone joining in on the chorus. Or, let different groups rehearse a verse each for a few minutes, before putting it all together, with everyone joining in on the chorus.

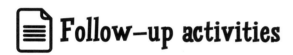 **Follow-up activities**

Weird and wonderful

- Once the class has an idea of the process, invite each group to write their verse – three lines, plus the last line *That's no place to put a pet*. To ensure the pets are not duplicated, assign each group their own specific list, or let them choose weird and wonderful animals as 'pets', such as elephants, skunks, dinosaurs and monkeys. All these will be fun and inspire creativity.

Story line

- Alternatively, you can extend the experience by turning each line into a story. For example, for *Don't put the cat in Grandma's hat*, ask:
  - What type of cat is it?
  - What's the cat's name?
  - Where was it?
  - Who put it in the hat?
  - What type of hat was it?
  - Where was Granny going in her hat?
  - What happened when the cat escaped from the hat?

- The answers to these questions can form the basis of the poem. Once drafted, look again for detail, exaggeration, humour, and good lines to repeat.

12 HAIKU

Haiku, originating in Japan, is a very precise form of poetry. A haiku has a total of 17 syllables and follows a specific line structure: line one has five syllables, line two has seven syllables, and line three has five syllables.

Haikus often try to 'paint a picture' or capture a moment. One of my favourites is 'Haiku' by Dr John Cooper Clarke (*Silly Poems* page 62). If possible, share this with the class. It highlights how hard it can be to write to the syllable limit – though you may have to explain the 'joke' to the children.

Read and perform

There are a variety of haikus in *Silly Poems*:

• 'Flu Haiku' by Clare Kirwan, page 65. This slightly disgusting but funny poem plays on the word *snot*, which children will, no doubt, find hilarious.

• 'IQ Haiku' by Trevor Parsons, page 67. Another amusing haiku with puns, which also highlights the haiku structure of *three lions* (lines) and *five silly bulls* (syllables).

• 'The Rapping Haiku' by John Foster, page 70. This haiku is slightly different in that it has three verses, incorporating rhythm and rhyme in each.

Read and perform the poems together, using the notes on page 6 to support you. As there are only 17 syllables in a haiku, it's important to emphasise each one and make the most of the few words that you have. Focus on any jokes or plays on words.

When performing and writing haikus, it's important to look at the structure of each line and the ways that these can be performed. For John Foster's 'The Rapping Haiku', you can make use of the internal rhymes to help you pick up the beat.

Discuss

• Explore the best speed to perform each line.
• Talk about how to emphasise the jokes and puns vocally.
• Consider the different tone of voice and expression in each haiku.

 ## Ideas for your own poems

Step 1

Before you start on your own haiku, write a few haiku examples on the board (see Read and perform). Read them out and invite the class to count the syllables on their fingers.

It's not often I suggest teaching rules for poetry, but a haiku must follow a specific structure to be a haiku (see above). So it's worth explaining the syllable structure.

A good way is to start with the children's names – go round the class and ask them to say their names out loud, counting the syllables in their names on their fingers. For example:

• Paul – one
• Sally – Sal/lee – two
• Ishmael – Ish/ma/el – three
• Annabella – Ann/a/bell/a – four

Step 2

Using their names as a starting point, invite them to write a haiku about themselves. They could focus on favourite foods, hobbies, clothes or interests. Keep it simple. For example:

> Paul likes to eat sweets
> Watches football on TV
> And plays loud music

Or maybe:

> Annabella sings
> loudly when she's in the bath
> and she has long hair

At the moment, you are concentrating on the structure (five–seven–five). Once you have that, you can look at adding extra detail and a wider vocabulary.

Step 3

Start by looking at the ones you've got and see if you can make them better or more interesting. So *Paul likes to eat sweets* is okay, but could be better.

Decide which are the most important words in this line (probably *Paul* and *sweets*). Then explore ways to make the other words better, funnier or more descriptive. For example:

> Paul likes eating sweets
> Paul likes sweet sweets
> Paul likes sticky sweets
> Paul loves sticky sweets
> Paul scoffs sticky sweets

All these lines say pretty much the same thing, but *scoffs sticky sweets* sounds good – the word *scoffs* is funny and adds to the alliteration.

Your first ideas are the ones that will get you going, but you can make them better. It's like driving in first gear – you can get to your destination, but it's much more fun if you go in a higher gear. The same applies to poems – the better the words, the better the poems. Remember the mantra, that poetry is about putting the best words in the best order. Try them in different orders to hear how they sound.

Repeat this process with each line.

Next try deleting words such as *and*, *then* and *so*. Poetry can exist in truncated phrases, letting our brains fill in the missing words. For example, *And she has long hair* is okay, but we can say so much more about the hair:

> Long wavy black hair

This gives more detail and removes *And she has* – we know *long wavy black hair* means that she has long wavy black hair.

Step 4

Move on to consider what else you can write a haiku about. It could be anything – descriptions of scenes, pictures, seasons, weather and so on.

Try using poems you have already written as a starting point. Take, for instance, a poem about animals from Workshop 6 (page 27):

> Trunk swinger
> Water squirter
> Ear flapper

Try adding words that end in 'ly'.

> Trunk swinging gently
> To and fro, squirting water
> While it flaps its ears

This sounds okay, but what about:

> Gently swinging trunk
> Squirting water in the air
> Ears flapping slowly

Does this sound better? Or maybe *water squirting in the air* sounds better. It's all about chipping away and seeing how far you can take the ideas.

There is something satisfying about trying to fit as much information, description or feeling into as few syllables as possible. Haikus are like little poetry postcards – simple and direct – and everyone can do them.

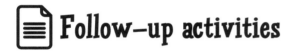 Follow-up activities

Adding more
- Don't stop at one verse – challenge your class to write two or three verses, building a fuller picture.

Create a scene
- Put up a display of famous paintings, scenes or photographs and invite the children to write haikus based on these.

Closer to home
- Ask the children to focus on family members or pets, drawing inspiration from home for their haikus.

13 FINDING THE BEST RHYME

Most children (and many adults) will think of rhyme when they think of poetry. There is something inherently satisfying about the sound of a good rhyme. I love it when I am writing my own poems and come up with a rhyme that sounds just right for the poem. It fits perfectly and is often fun.

Children are often keen to make their poems rhyme, but those rhymes don't always work. It's been said before, but is worth repeating – the rhyme must fit the poem, not the poem fit around the rhyme. So, we are going to look at rhymes and how to get the best rhymes. This will be good preparation for writing limericks in the next workshop.

Read and perform
There are a variety of rhyming poems, such as:

● 'The King of All the Dinosaurs' by Paul Cookson from *Dinosaur Poems*, page 19. This descriptive poem uses repetition and rhyme to build up a highly visual image of the fearsome Tyrannosaurus rex.

● 'Dragon Dance' by Max Fatchen from *Magic Poems*, pages 78–79. This poem celebrates the dance of the ferocious Chinese dragon through the streets at New Year.

● 'My Gran' by Moira Andrew from *Family Poems*, pages 44–45. This heart-warming poem depicts a grandmother using an increasing number of rhyming descriptions.

Read and perform the poems together, using the notes on page 6 to support you. When reading and performing these poems, it will be very important to get the correct rhythm and speed for each poem. Practise a few times until it feels right and you feel confident.

Discuss
● Ask the class which rhymes they liked best?

● Can they suggest which rhymes worked best and why? Were there any unusual or particularly effective rhymes?

● Do they think the rhymes helped the humour of the poems?

● Ask if rhymes always occur at the end of a line. Then take a look at examples of different rhyming patterns and structures:

   ● Four-line verses, with lines two and four rhyming
   ● Rhyming couplets
   ● Single rhymes for a verse or poem
   ● Internal rhymes
   ● Made-up or joke rhymes

 Ideas for your own poems

Step 1

Getting the right rhyme is fundamental to a poem – it can be time-consuming but is worth doing. Choosing the word to rhyme with is important. If it's a difficult rhyme then it makes the task even harder. The following rhyming exercise should help.

Let's start with a phrase from Workshop 10, which lists what the children do when the teacher is out of the room:

> When the teacher isn't there

The word *there* is a good word to rhyme with. So start by writing the alphabet vertically down the side of the board. Tell the children to do the same in their books. Then go through the alphabet and find words to rhyme with *there*. Write a few on the board, then give the class five minutes to write their own (individually or in pairs) and share these on the board. For example:

A – air, aware, affair
B – bare, bear, beware
C – care, chair, Claire
D – dare, deckchair, derrière
E – eclair
F – flare, flair, fair, fare
G – glare
H – hair, her
I – incur, impair
L – lair

Step 2

Then go through the rhymes and pick the ones that fit the subject of the poem and make sense. For example:

> Paper planes in the **air**
> Pencils flying in the **air**

Aware is a difficult and awkward word to fit naturally at the end of a phrase. Something like *Everybody is aware* rhymes but doesn't sound quite right – there are better options.

> Someone cuddles a teddy **bear**

While this rhymes, it isn't the sort of naughty thing that happens when the teacher isn't there.

> Jason growls like a grizzly **bear**
> Jason shows his bottom **bare**
> Jason's bottom – big and **bare**

These better fit the subject of the poem – the second is funnier than the first, but the third sounds right. *Beware* is a good rhyme and subject match, *deckchair* should be on the beach so is not right, *impair* is not usually a word that children use, whereas *chair*, *care* and *fair* are.

Step 3

Once you have identified some rhymes that work, look at building up a line that fits. Together, say the phrase:

> When / the / teac/her / is/n't / there
> De / de / de / de / de / de / de

Ask the children to pick a word that fits and then write a line to go along with it. Go round the class, asking children to say them out loud (or say them out loud for them). Emphasise the rhythm so they can decide whether they work. For example:

> Jason growls like a grizzly bear

This is okay and fits but is not the exact rhythm.

TIP *Writing new lines based on a set number of syllables isn't a hard and fast rule. Go by what sounds and feels best.*

> *Jason's like a grizzly bear*

This fits the beat perfectly, but has lost the *growl* and the alliteration with it. The name can be changed to just one syllable:

> *John growls like a grizzly bear*

Or maybe just:

> *Growling like a grizzly bear*

Paper planes in the air only has six beats, but by emphasising the words in certain ways it sounds okay:

> *Pa/per / planes [pause] in / the / air*

Though this simpler version is better:

> *Paper planes fly through the air*

 Step 4

Put the lines together in verses of four lines, with the fourth line being *When the teacher isn't there*. Because this is not a narrative poem and has no story, the order can be random and still work. However, you might want to group the lines together thematically:

> *Paper planes fly through the air*
> *John growls like a grizzly bear*
> *We don't mind and we don't care*
> *When the teacher isn't there*

 TIP *Don't be afraid of a noisy class. The best way to find out whether a poem works or not is to try it out loud.*

Let the children work in pairs or small groups to do this.

📄 Follow-up activities

Start it off

- Give the class a variety of lines to start them off and repeat the process with different rhymes:

> *There's something on my pencil case*
> *What's that noise behind the door?*
> *When my brother eats baked beans*

14 LIMERICKS

Short, tight, rhythmic and often funny – there is something perfect about a good limerick. Because they are only five lines, they appear easy to write. And because they are funny, they are an attractive proposition. However, getting the best rhymes can sometimes be tricky and time consuming – but worth it!

Limericks typically have five lines. Lines one, two and five rhyme with each other and have the same verbal rhythm (usually seven to ten syllables). Lines three and four also rhyme with each other and have the same verbal rhythm (usually five to seven syllables).

Read and perform

There are a variety of limericks, such as:

• The collection of 'Loopy Limericks' from *Silly Poems*, pages 85–96. This selection of 11 limericks use humour, word play and, of course, rhyme.

• 'There Once Was a Schoolboy From Florida' by Dr John Cooper Clarke from *Disgusting Poems*, page 1. This funny limerick describes the results of a flatulent school child.

• 'There Was an Old Man From Darjeeling' from *Disgusting Poems*, page 49. This perverse limerick recounts the tale of a man who spits on the ceiling instead of the floor of a bus.

Read and perform the poems together, using the notes on page 6 to support you. The rhythmic nature of the limerick is obviously important – it's almost sing-song. Equally important though is the performance of the final line, as this is often where the pay-off, joke or twist occurs, so it needs to be clear.

Discuss

• Draw the children's attention to the rhythms and structures of the limericks. Can they see any similarities? (Many have a name in the first line.)

• If possible, share Dr John Cooper Clarke's 'Limerick on How to Write a Limerick' from *Silly Poems*, page 1. This clever limerick describes the rules to write a limerick.

 ## Ideas for your own poems

Step 1

Spend a bit of time reading the limericks out so that the children get a feel for their rhythm. To write a limerick, they will need to understand how they feel and work.

Help them to focus on the rhythm by speaking out the rhythm for the class to repeat or join in with:

> De de de de de de de de
> De de de de de de de de
> De de de de de
> De de de de de
> De de de de de de de de

Step 2

Start by writing the first line of the limerick. They often begin:

> There once was fellow called [insert rhyming name]
> There once was a lady from [insert rhyming place name]

You could try the name of a town or place, but it might be easier to start with their names. Not every name will rhyme – if so they can either choose to use an abbreviation, an initial or choose another name that rhymes more easily.

> **TIP**
> Be aware that some rhymes inevitably lead to cheeky words. You may have to find ways of deflecting this. Some rhymes you will just need to avoid!

Go round the class and use a few names as examples. Try to explain which ones might work better than others and why. For example, lots of things rhyme with the 'all' sound:

> There was a young fellow called Paul

Whichever name you start with, you will only need three good rhymes for the limerick. Go through the alphabet (as in Workshop 13) and choose the best rhymes. If you were using *Paul* you could use rhymes such as *all, ball, call, hall, tall, small* and *wall*. These all have potential – so you could have:

> **TIP**
> Bear in mind where the last line might be going at this stage. Was he kicking it over the *wall*? Were his football boots too *small*? Did he smash the light in the *hall*?

> There once was a boy called Paul
> Who was always kicking a ball

Children might be tempted to put *football*, but the *football* is quite difficult to work into the rhythm of the line.

Step 3

The middle two lines of the limerick are shorter, must rhyme with each other and need to keep the 'story' going.

It's a good idea to know what the last line is likely to be as that will give the poem some direction.

If the last line is *And broke all the lights in the hall*, then the middle two lines should be about playing football in the house.

However, if the last line is *But kicked it over the wall*, then the middle two lines should take place in the garden.

Equally, if the last line is *But his shorts were tight and too small*, the middle lines should mention other parts of the kit as well.

Remember these lines are shorter, so keep the rhymes simple. For example:

> There once was a boy called Paul
> Who was always kicking a ball
> It bounced on the floor
> Smashed on the door
> And broke all the lights in the hall

There once was a boy called Paul
Who was always kicking a ball
Outside on the grass
His dad tried to pass
But kicked it over the wall

There once was a boy called Paul
Who was always kicking a ball
His shirt was too long
It fitted King Kong
But his shorts were tight and too small

Much of this will be trial and error – sometimes they'll get it, sometimes not. If they're struggling, read some out in class and work collaboratively to improve them.

Some limericks repeat the first line at the end. If anyone is finding it particularly difficult, this can be a good solution.

Step 4

Once children are confident with the limerick structure, let them try using place names instead.

Discuss which sort of place names would work best. Look at countries:
- Spain – pain, again, rain, mane
- America – not much!
- Germany – (exaggerate the 'ee' in *Germanee*) family, carefully, cheerfully, carpentry
- China – finer, miner, designer, shiner

You'll probably find it's the shorter names that have more potential.

Try towns and places, too:
- Dundee – me, see, tree, degree, flee
- Preston – (you might have to combine words) rest on, vest on, messed on
- London – undone, but not much else

So, as you can see, making the choice for the first line is the most important decision.

If you feel really brave, you could let them use teachers' surnames.

 TIP Think ahead and come up with places and names that are easy to rhyme with, and maybe also provide children with a few possible rhymes.

Follow-up activities

Serious stuff
- Challenge the children to have a go at writing limericks that are not humorous.

Natural inspiration
- If possible, share 'The Year in Limericks' by Eric Finney from *Silly Poems*, page 94. Encourage the children to try writing limericks about animals.

15 TONGUE TWISTERS AND ALLITERATION

Tongue twisters are great fun to try out loud as someone will inevitably get them wrong, with humorous results. Also, most children will be familiar with well-known tongue twisters, such as 'She Sells Sea Shells', 'Peter Piper', 'Betty Botter', 'Red Lorry, Yellow Lolly' and so on.

Read and perform

The collection of 'Tricky Tongue Twisters' from *Silly Poems*, pages 49–60. This selection of ten tricky-to-say poems play with language and present difficult word combinations that give humorous results.

Read and perform the poems together, using the notes on page 6 to support you. Tongue twisters by their very nature are difficult to read and say, but this is also their strength and attraction. Being able to say it without going wrong is something to aim for – but getting it wrong will also provide lots of fun, too!

Discuss

• Have a class discussion about what makes a good tongue twister. Can the children suggest which letters lend themselves to tongue twisters the best? Which type of sounds are they? Talk about consonants working better than vowels and discuss if some consonants are better than others.

• Invite the children to talk about which poems they liked best and why.

 ## Ideas for your own poems

 Step 1

Ask the class, if they were to write their own tongue twister, which letters would work best?

Go through the alphabet and consider each letter. Focus on consonants rather than vowels – there will be some consonants that will be more effective. Refer back to tongue twisters they are familiar with, such as 'She Sells Sea Shells' and so on.

Make a list on the board of those letters that would work best.

 Step 2

Take one of the famous tongue twisters as a starting point, such as 'She Sells Sea Shells'. Firstly, think of a boy's name and girl's name that begin with the same sound, such as:

> Shaun and Sally

Then add the tongue twister (I've rearranged the words slightly – you'll see why and can do this with the others too):

> Shaun and Sally the seashore shell sellers

Say it out loud for the class to repeat, or say it together. Then change the names around, so the next line will be:

> Sally and Shaun the seashore shell sellers

Say both lines. Then swap the beginning and end around:

> The seashore shell sellers – Shaun and Sally

Say all three lines.

Ask the children to look at the pattern so far and guess what the next line will be. Some may have spotted this:

> The seashore shell sellers – Sally and Shaun

Say all four lines. It's starting to get complicated but is also fun to remember and to try to say out loud.

Next, just use one name:

> Shaun – the seashore shell seller

Then ask the class to guess the next line:

> Sally – the seashore shell seller

Say these six lines together and let them predict what the last two lines will be:

> The seashore shell seller – Shaun
> The seashore shell seller – Sally

Step 3

Put the whole verse together:

> Shaun and Sally the seashore shell sellers
> Sally and Shaun the seashore shell sellers
> The seashore shell sellers – Shaun and Sally
> The seashore shell sellers – Sally and Shaun
> Shaun – the seashore shell seller
> Sally – the seashore shell seller
> The seashore shell seller – Shaun
> The seashore shell seller – Sally

This is a great way of showing how to get an eight-line tongue twister from one line, where no lines are the same and no extra words are used. It really shows what you can do with one line.

Once you've done this as a class, invite the children to try it either individually or in pairs.

> **TIP** Give the children examples of possible titles or opening lines. They can use these if they want to, or think of their own.

Based on well-known tongue twisters, opening lines could include:

> The pickled pepper pickers
> The better butter biters
> The red lorry riders
> The yellow lolly lickers

Or create new combinations, such as:

> The mad marshmallow munchers
> The bubble gum blowers
> The lollipop lickers
> The big belching burpers
> The silly song singers
> The fantastic flan flingers
> The great gobstopper gobblers
> The jumping gerbil jugglers
> The twisting tongue twisters

Invite the class to think of two names beginning with appropriately tricky letters, which they can use to write their own eight-line tongue twisters.

Step 4

Now start to build up your tongue twister. Ask the children to think of other words beginning with 's' or 'sh' that could describe shells.

Write their ideas on the board, such as *shiny*, *sandy*, *salty*, *sharp*, *smelly*, *sparkly*, *stinky*, *slippy*, *small*, *shimmering*, *shining* and *sliced*. Then add these to the original poem:

> Shaun sells shiny shells
> Sally sells sandy shells
> Shaun sells shiny sharp shells
> Sally sells sandy smelly shells
>
> Shauns's shells are small and stinky
> Sally's shells are slippy, sparkly and shimmering

📄 Follow-up activities

Creative collections

● Tongue twisters are often short, so try creating a set of themed tongue twisters, such as a countdown of tongue twisters:

> Ten twisting…
> Nine new…

● Seasonal tongue twisters:

> When it's winter Wendy…
> Since spring sprung Sue…

● Sporting tongue twisters:

> Fantastic football…
> Terrific tennis…

● And celebrations or special times of the year tongue twisters, such as for birthdays, Halloween, Bonfire Night, Christmas, Divali, Mother's Day and Father's Day.

16 SPELLS

Many spells and recipes are lists and, as many of these workshops show, lists are a great way to start the ideas process. In this workshop we will look at how to get the best out of our lists to form a spell-based poem.

Read and perform

'Double, Double, Toil and Trouble' by William Shakespeare from *Magic Poems*, pages 60–61. This classic extract from *Macbeth* sets a dark undertone, as the three witches add loathsome ingredients to create their *hell-broth*.

An extract from *The Witch's Work Song* by TH White from *Magic Poems*, page 69. In contrast to the previous extract, this is a rather joyful account of a witch's brew, made with fantastical and magical ingredients.

Read and perform the poems together, using the notes on page 6 to support you. Both these poems lend themselves to dramatic performance. Rhythm and rhyme play a strong role but there is also opportunity for great expression when describing the ingredients – have fun with this! Also, you can try reading more slowly with lots of emphasis on the disgusting or unpleasant items.

Discuss

- As a class, look together at the rhythms and the structure of each poem.
- Discuss which lines the children think work best and why.
- Explain that both these spells have ingredients. Which ingredients are the most popular with the class? Have a vote and discuss the results.

 Ideas for your own poems

Step 1

Challenge the children to come up with a list of ingredients. Write these on the board. Point out that animals and their body parts feature strongly in both the example poems, as do plants. You can also include foods, things from school – anything really. Encourage specific, singular items, such as *a cat's eye* and *a dog's tooth*, rather than *cats* and *dogs*.

For example: *cat's eye, lumpy custard, sweaty socks, rat's tail, slimy beans, dad's pants, nettle stings, toilet roll, tooth of a dog, earwax, teacher's shoe, shark's fins, Grandad's toe, frog's legs.*

Step 2

You can perform this list straight away, by saying it out loud for the class to repeat and exaggerating the rhythms:

> Cat's – eye – lump–y – cus–tard
> Swea–ty – socks – rat's – tail
> Sli–my – beans – dad's – pants
> Nett–le – stings – toi–let – roll
> Tooth – of – a – dog – ear–wax
> Tea–cher's – shoe – shark's – fins
> Gran–dad's – toe – frog's – legs

This will work fine and sound great, but you can make it better by looking to see if there are any rhymes already in the list, or if there are any words that could lead to good rhymes. For example:

> Nettle stings – shark's fins

Both *cat* and *rat* and *dog* and *frog* rhyme, so if you change the order you could have:

> Eye of cat – tail of rat
> Tooth of a dog – leg of a frog

This also makes it sound more like a spell.

Then try to pick out the words that could have good rhymes.

- Tail – snail, whale, ale, scale
- Beans – greens, tangerines, cream
- Roll – mole, toilet bowl, hole, pole, vole

These will give you other potential lines, such as:

> Rat's tail – slime from a snail / skin of a whale / dragon's scale / rancid ale
> Slimy beans – curried greens / tangerines / mouldy cream
> Toilet roll – claws of a mole / toilet bowl / half a hole / nose of a vole

TIP

The rhymes don't have to be exact, as long as they are good enough when they are said aloud.

They sound good when chanted. Let the class choose the ones that they like best.

Step 3

You still have all the ones that don't rhyme as well, so you can put them together and use all the ideas. Set it out on the board like this and then fill in the gaps:

> nettle stings
> shark's fins
> eye of cat
> tail of rat
> tooth of a dog
> leg of a frog
> slimy beans
> mouldy cream

Write ingredients that don't rhyme but fit the rhythm on the left. There are no right or wrong answers here – just whichever fit best. So you could have:

> Lumpy custard – nettle stings
> Sweaty socks – shark's fins
> Dad's pants – eye of cat
> Earwax – tail of rat
> Teacher's shoe – tooth of a dog
> Grandad's toe – leg of a frog
> [Something else] – slimy beans
> [Something else] – mouldy cream

TIP

I sometimes say **something else** (or **something that fits**) just to show the class that anything can go here – that it's the rhythm that's important.

If you use all the ideas from the initial set, you will then need to come up with some more ideas to fit. For example: *sister's doll, slug slime, bat's wing* (actually *bat's wing* may be better than *shark's fin*, so you could swap them), *football boot*:

> Lumpy custard – nettle sting(s) [take off the 's']
> Sweaty socks – bat's wing
> Dad's pants – eye of cat
> Earwax – tail of rat
> Teacher's shoe – tooth of a dog
> Grandad's toe – leg of a frog
> Slug slime – slimy beans
> Football boot – mouldy cream

Having *slug slime* and *slimy beans* on the same line is a bit much though, so you could swap the rhyming item for one of the other options, such as *curried beans* or *cold baked beans*:

> Slug slime – curried beans
> Football boot – mouldy cream

Step 4

It is now time to decide how the potion or spell is applied and what it is a spell for. As a class, discuss how and where the spell will be mixed, how often it should be applied, how it will be applied and so on.

You only need a couple of lines here, so you might have something like this:

> All stirred up with a great big stick
> Twice a day – spread on thick

Or maybe something simple and funny:

> Cook it all in Grandad's bed
> Pour it over Grandad's head

If you want, you can give the class an opening line, such as:

> A most exotic potion
> A strange and weird lotion

Put all the lines together and you have:

> A most exotic potion
> A strange and weird lotion
> Lumpy custard – nettle sting
> Sweaty socks – bat's wing
> Dad's pants – eye of cat
> Earwax – tail of rat
> Teacher's shoe – tooth of a dog
> Grandad's toe – leg of a frog
> Slug slime – curried beans
> Football boot – mouldy cream
> All stirred up with a great big stick
> Twice a day – spread on thick

Finally, decide as a class what it is a spell for. It could be:

> A spell to make a teacher smile
> A spell to get dad's hair to grow
> A spell to make the school dinners taste better
> A spell to shrink your big brother

Once you're in agreement, you'll have a title – and a poem.

Follow-up activities

Matching ingredients

- Challenge the class to think of appropriate ingredients for different types of spells. For example, a funny spell will need funny words and ingredients, a spooky spell will need spooky ingredients, and a spell for school will need school-based ingredients.

Special spells

- Focus the spell casting on specific occasions (such as Christmas, Divali or different seasons) or goals (such as making you better at football, dancing, maths or singing).

Adding detail

- Once the class have got the idea of building up the poem, encourage them to add detail. Explore what happened after – did the potion work? Did it fail? If so, what happened? Maybe the potion was used on the wrong person, or the pet dog. See where their ideas take you!

THE MONSTER IN OUR SCHOOL

In this workshop, you are going to ask the children a series of different questions about a monster in their school. Their answers, which can be as detailed as possible, will form the basis of their poem.

Read and perform

There are a variety of poems about creatures and monsters in *Spooky Poems*. For example, 'It' by Eric Finney from *Spooky Poems*, pages 72–73. This gentle poem builds an eerie dread as it describes the devastation in the wake of a nameless, oozing creature from the sea.

Read and perform the poems together, using the notes on page 6 to support you. Emphasise the strong rhythm and rhyme, as well as the repetition of *It* – this will help punctuate the poem.

Discuss

- Look at the structure of the poem together. Ask the children which lines they think worked well and why. Do they have any favourites?
- Focus on the rhymes and rhythm.
- Ask how the repetition of *It* helps the poem. Does it make a difference having *It* at the beginning of each line? Does *It* make it sound spookier than if the monster had a name? Can they explain why?

 ## Ideas for your own poems

 Step 1

Ask the children to imagine there is a creature in your school. At this stage, it is important to state that you don't know what it is. If you decide it's a vampire or a werewolf or a ghost, it will confine your ideas. You are going to build up a picture of it a bit at a time.

 TIP I usually make a rule that it's not a violent creature – it doesn't eat teachers, suck their blood, kill dinner ladies or so on. It can be scary and spooky, but it's not a killer. It's good to do this at the outset so the children don't get drawn into the bloodthirsty nature of the beast.

Write some questions on the board for the children. Ask them to write down their answers – these will form the starting points for their poems.

The first questions are about the creature itself:

1. Where in the school does the creature live?
Try and think of somewhere no one else will think of.

2. When does it come out?
Day or night? What time of day or night? In what type of weather? Only in certain lessons?

3. Who sees it?
Just you? All the class? Only the teachers? Only the dinner ladies or the cleaners? No one?

4. How does it move?
Does it fly? Slither? Hop? Bounce? Teleport? Swim through pipes?

5. What noises does it make?

The noises could be the sounds it makes itself, or they could sound like noises that might be heard in school, such as creaky doors and so on.

Give the children enough time to write their ideas down. Don't worry too much about handwriting and spelling at this stage – these can be corrected later.

You could make a writing frame for the children to fill in if they have trouble with writing.
For example:

- It lives…
- It comes out when…
- It is seen by…

> **TIP**
> The children will want to discuss their ideas. I usually suggest they write them down first and discuss them later – this will give more focus to their writing.

Step 2

Move on to think about some other aspects of the creature:

6. What does it eat?

Maybe strange mixtures of food and things found in school – chips, pencils and homework.

> **TIP**
> Children often suggest that it eats from the toilet. This may be pretty funny, but if you want to deflect from this you can say that if everyone puts that then it won't be original or funny. I also tend to say that it doesn't eat flesh or people either.

7. What does it drink?

Again, it doesn't drink from the toilet! But it might drink liquids found around the school, such as red paint, glue, cold coffee, sweat from socks, liquidised test papers.

8. What does it do when it comes out?

Does it play tricks on the children or the teacher? Does it help with homework? Or hide things? Or get you into trouble? Ask the children to write down three things that it does.

9. What is its name?

Names of characters that already exist cannot be used, such as Dracula, Frankenstein, Eewok or Dementor. Also, it's best to stay away from the names of other members of the class or other teachers.

Here are a couple of strategies for finding a name:

- See if there is something in the list that suggests a name. For example, if the monster is thin, maybe *Bones* would work well.

- Alternatively, ask the children to write their names backwards or mix up the letters to make new and weird words. *Paul* could become *Luap*, and *Martin* could be *Nitram*. Some names, such as *Lucy*, may not work as well, or so it would seem. But if you spell them backwards and say them phonetically (*Ye-cull*), they might work better.

Step 3

Once you have all the ideas, you need to turn them into a poem. Here are a few suggestions how to do this.

- Read out the answers from questions 1 to 9.

> It lives in the stock cupboard
> It comes out at 4.15 when everyone has gone home
> Only the cleaners see the creature…

- Read out the answers but change the order around.

> Bones comes out at midnight
> Eats all the teacher's chocolates mixed with homework
> Bounces down the corridor…

- Read the answers with the name of the creature at the beginning of every line or pair of lines.

> Bones lives in the stock cupboard
> And bounces down the corridor
>
> Bones comes out straight after school
> Only the cleaners see the creature

- Read it out forwards, then repeat it reversed. It's a great trick – the children can pretend they have done twice as much work.

> It lives in the corridor
> In the corridor…It lives
>
> It bounces on the tables
> On the tables…It bounces

- Play around with repetition – it can be very effective.

> It lives in the corridor
> Lives in the corridor
> Lives in the corridor
> And comes out after school
>
> It bounces on the tables
> Bounces on the tables
> Bounces on the tables
> Boing boing boing !

- Take a couple of the children's favourite ideas or lines and make them into a chorus. Have a verse, then a chorus and so on – the verse can be different line lengths.

> Boing Boing Boing
> Bouncing down the corridor

Step 4

Once the children have written a first or second draft, ask them to read them out loud. Based on their reading out and the sound of the words, suggest changes or good lines to repeat. If anything doesn't work or sound good, suggest they take it out.

Encourage the children to write in phrases rather than repeating *It* in every line. For example:

> It lives in the corridor
> Bounces on the tables
> Eats all the teacher's chocolate
> Chews all the homework
> Spits out all the SATs

Notice here, also, different words for *eat* to add some variation of pace and vocabulary.

Follow-up activities

Break it up

● Invite the children to extend the poem or rewrite it so that every question becomes a verse or even a poem in its own right. Challenge them to think about details that can be added to make the poem more interesting.

A day in the life

● Let the children create a new poem based on the adventures of their creature. For example:
  ● The Day the Creature Ate the Homework
  ● The Day the Monster Burped in Class
  ● When the Creature Frightened Our Teacher

18 LISTS

As we've already seen, lists are a great starting point for any poem. In this workshop you are going to explore how lists can be used to best effect as well as how to extend them.

Read and perform

The collection of 'Loopy Lists' from *Silly Poems*, pages 39–48. This selection of eight poems combine humour with wordplay in this joyfully simple format.

Read and perform the poems together, using the notes on page 6 to support you. Some of these poems rely heavily on rhythm and rhyme. Others are based more on puns, involving wordplay and jokes – think about the best ways to emphasise these to get the best laughs.

Discuss

- Talk about the different features of the example list poems, such as alphabets, rhymes, puns.
- Find out which ones are the most popular and why.

  Ideas for your own poems

Step 1

Tell the class you are going to write a poem titled 'Things to Find in the Teacher's Bag'. This will be a cartoon-type poem, so anything can happen. Explain that the bag is bigger on the inside than it looks, so big things can fit inside it.

Ask the children to suggest what is in the bag and write the list down the left-hand side of the board:

- Pens
- Headache tablets
- Chocolate bars
- Car keys
- Mobile phones
- Planning sheets
- Confiscated toys

Once you have a list, it can be performed by giving it rhythm and adding an introduction and chorus:

> Things to find, things to find
> Things to find in a teacher's bag
>
> Pens, headache tablets
> Chocolate bars, car keys
> Mobile phones, planning sheets
> Confiscated toys
>
> Things to find, things to find
> Things to find in a teacher's bag

Divide the class into groups and invite each to write a verse, as in previous workshops. Build on the principles you have used so far – adding rhymes or focusing each verse on a specific theme, such as school items, food, wallet or money.

Step 2

Once you have done this as a class exercise, ask the children to write their own 'Things to Find…' list. So they are not all the same, give them a range of possible titles to base their poems on:

- Things to Find Under Brother's Bed
- Things to Find in the Dog's Basket
- Things to Find in a Pirate's Pocket
- Things to Find in a Magician's Hat
- Things to Find in a Monster's Stomach
- Things to Find in a Dragon's Cave
- Things to Find in an Alien Spaceship
- Things to Find in the Changing Rooms After a Football Match

Either let them choose, or have them on folded sheets and give them out randomly. Ensure there are equal numbers of each category.

Give the class about ten minutes of quiet writing time to write their list. Make sure they write the list down the left-hand side of their page.

Step 3

Once they have their list, explain that they are going to add detail to it to make it more interesting. This is why the list is written down the left-hand side. Go down the list and invite the children to describe the items.

> **TIP** *Encourage exaggeration – a teacher may have five pens in their bag but 100 pens, with the lids off and ink congealed sounds much better.*

So you could end up with ideas such as these:

- Pens – 100 pens, tops off, congealed ink that's blobbed on the work
- Headache tablets – lots of empty packets of headache tablets, crinkled boxes, powder crumbs
- Chocolate bars – 1000 eaten chocolate bars, scrunched-up foil, bits of melted chocolate smudged on the school reports
- Car keys
- Mobile phones
- Planning sheets
- Confiscated toys
- False teeth

> **TIP** *You don't have to add detail to everything on the list – just the ones that work well and lend themselves to it. You won't be using all the ideas – focus on the best words and best ideas.*

Step 4

Put the ideas together into a poem. Start with the title and then the list of items and their descriptions – start with the ordinary or obvious ones and work up to the unusual and funnier ones.

Then divide the list into verses and include an opening line for each verse. For example:

> Inside the teacher's bag are strange things,
> [Choose two, three or four items from the list]
>
> Inside the teacher's bag are strange things,
> Very strange things like…
> [Add another two, three or four items from the list]
>
> Inside the teacher's bag are strange things,
> Very, very strange things…
> [Add another two, three or four items from the list]

Encourage the children to think of a reason why they might be looking in this place and finding these things. Add this detail to the opening section. For example:

> Miss had confiscated my football
> Just because I was playing it in class
> I saw it disappear inside her bag.
> I waited until she went to the staffroom at break
> For her cup of coffee and chocolate cake
> And making sure that no one was around
> I gently put my hand into the bag…
> You'll never guess what I found.
> There were…
> [Add some items from the list]
>
> I still couldn't find my football
> It had disappeared into the black hole
> That is my teacher's bag
> With the…
> [Add more items from the list]

Follow-up activities

Picking favourites

● Ask the class which are their favourite ideas from their lists. Can they suggest which have most potential for detail and extension? Encourage them to focus on one of these for the whole poem. It could be something like:

- The Forgotten Lunch in Miss Morgan's Bag
- Mr Stephenson's Football Kit
- The Lost Lessons of Miss Hill

Monstrous baggage

● Suggest that the bag could be an alien or a monster from outer space. Give the children ideas such as:

- The Bag That Eats the Homework
- I Think My Teacher's Bag Is Alive
- The Day That Jonathan Disappeared

● Follow their ideas and see where they take you.

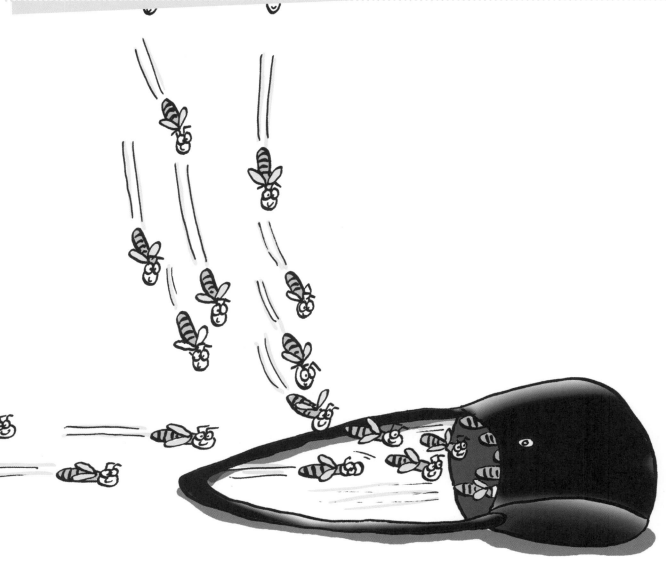

19 FAMILIES AND THEIR HABITS

Previous workshops have focused on poems about brothers and sisters – this workshop is based on other members of the family (parents, step-parents, grandparents, aunties and uncles).

Read and perform

'My Gran' by Moira Andrew from *Family Poems*, pages 44–45. This thoughtful and sentimental poem describing *Gran* gradually builds on its own structure and pattern, extending the rhythm and rhymes but always coming back to the line *kind of gran*.

Read and perform the poem together using the notes on page 6 to support you. Focus on the rhymes and try to get the best out of these when you perform it. Look particularly at the last line in each verse and how to pace it.

Discuss

- Have a class discussion about the structure of the poem.
- Point out that the layout is unusual but interesting. Ask if this affects the way it's performed.

  ## Ideas for your own poems

Step 1

Ask the children to answer the questions below. Give them plenty of examples and plenty of time to write the answers down. Most of the answers will just be single words or phrases. They don't need to think of entire poems at the moment – just focus on their ideas.

Ask them to decide who they are writing about and then answer these questions:

1. What do they look like?

- Short, tall, fat, thin
- Grey hair, no hair
- Big nose, massive hands, tiny ears, and so on

For example, if I was thinking of my own grandad I would say: *bald head, long sideburns, thick glasses, four chins, naval tattoos on his arms, beer belly.*

2. What habits do they have? What do they always do?

- Crack their knuckles
- Rub their ears
- Fiddle with their hair, ears, nose
- Sit in a certain way on the sofa
- Clean their glasses
- Stick their tongue out of the side of their mouth when they're concentrating
- Rub your face with his whiskers when he hasn't shaved
- Give you an embarrassing hair ruffle or kiss?

TIP

I usually suggest that children don't write about brothers and sisters but somebody older. There's often more to write about and their relationships are more emotionally interesting.

3. What do they always say?

These could be general sayings such as:

- Turn that music down
- Put the kettle on
- Have you done your homework?
- Things were different when we were young, we never had mobile phones or computers

They might be local phrases and colloquialisms, such as:

- Were you born in a barn?
- Put wood in th'ole
- Ey up me duck
- Nah then

This can include anything that they say regularly – the pet names they call the children, what their dad says when he's watching television, and so on.

Discuss these as a class, encouraging them to share and comment.

TIP It doesn't matter if children have more ideas for some sections than others. By the time you have finished and shared the ideas as a class, they will start to bounce ideas off each other and there will be more than enough for the poem.

Not only will this be lots of fun, but it is also a lovely way to show that though we are all different, there are many thing we will have in common. Poetry can help us remember and relate to these small details that can mean a lot.

Step 2

Ask a few more questions to add more detail:

4. Are there clothes they wear a lot? Do you picture them in a certain outfit?

- A favourite football or band T-shirt
- A favourite pair of jeans or boots

Grandparents or great-grandparents may look very similar:

- Matching brown tartan slippers
- Matching woolly pullovers

Maybe there's a particular set of clothes that this person wore on a particular occasion:

- That awful suit for your cousin's wedding
- That dress that was too tight

I always picture my grandad in a Hawaiian shirt, baggy cream trousers, sandals and socks. Not that he wore them all the time, but as they lived in Eastbourne we mostly saw them in the summer holidays.

5. What are their hobbies and interests? What are they obsessed by?

- A mad football fan
- Always in the shed mending things
- Collecting ornaments and other strange things
- Always on the internet
- Mad on exercise
- Always knitting a jumper for Christmas
- Always baking

6. What places do you associate with this person?

- A geographical place
- A holiday place or where they live
- The shed or greenhouse they spend most of their time
- The kitchen where they bake the best apple pies
- A favourite chair in front of the television
- Where they sit and read
- Somewhere associated with a particular occasion – a football stadium or theme park

7. Do you have any special memories of this person?

- Things done together

These could be funny, thoughtful or even sad – especially if the person they are writing about is no longer alive. Encourage them to share their ideas, thoughts, memories and emotions.

There are many ways to put the poem together. Try starting with the answers to the first question. Read the list out and then add a phrase like *That's my grandad* at the end of each section or verse.

If their grandma or grandad are known as Gramps, Nana, Granny Doreen, Grandad Jim and so on, use these names. It makes the poem more personal.

So if the poem was about my grandad, the first verse would be something like this:

> Bald head, long sideburns
> Thick glasses, four chins
> Beer belly and naval tattoos
> That's my grandad
>
> Always reading the sports page
> Sat in his favourite chair
> Walks round the house
> With his glasses perched on his bald head
> Looking for his glasses
> That's my grandad

Encourage the children to write in phrases rather than sentences. *Bald head, long sideburns* sounds better than *He has a bald head and he has long sideburns.*

Alternatively, instead of starting with looks, start with the section you have most answers for, is the funniest, or the most poignant. Again, have a repeated phrase at the end of each verse, such as *That's just Nana.*

Read them out to each other and see which lines or sections get the best responses. Ask the children which they can make more of. Can they think of any other phrases that sound good and could be repeated and built into the poem?

Follow-up activities

Focus in

● The very first time I led this workshop I ended up writing a poem about my father's hands – mainly because the Year 10 class in Bradford said they'd write a poem if I did! 'Father's Hands' turned into one of my favourite and most-appreciated pieces over the years.

● The questions will provide so many answers, any of which can be used to form an entire poem. If the children really take to this, encourage them to focus on just one or two answers as the main thrust of the poem, using the rest of the information as background.

● One of the memories might form the basis of the poem, such as Grandad in his shed. Invite them to describe the shed, what he does in it, the smells, the feel of things.

● Challenge them to add detail. For instance, saying that Grandad wears the same cap all the time is fine, but what colour is it? Brown? What type of brown? Patterned or plain? Old or new? Does he wear it at a funny angle? Does he wear it inside the house? Does Grandma tell him off?

TIP Tell the children to imagine that they're looking at this person through a telescope or a pair of binoculars from a distance. Once they have them in sight, they need to focus in to look at the small details.

20 MEMORIES

Memories are great starting points for poems, as they already exist – they don't have to be created from nothing. Often, the best memories are those of shared experiences, those memories that we have in common and that reflect our own experiences. In this workshop you will focus on a particular place and a particular memory.

Read and perform

'The Demon-Tree' by Jo Vernillo from *Spooky Poems*, pages 86–87. This nostalgic and reassuring poem describes a child's memory of a creepy tree that they feared but learned to appreciate.

Read and perform the poems together, using the notes on page 6 to support you. Consider the way the poem builds up when performing it. When you read it out loud, don't read it too quickly but savour the images and the feel of the words, building up the tension.

Discuss

- Look at the structure of the poem as a class. How is it laid out?
- Consider the lack of rhyme. What affect does this have?
- Focus on the build up of emotion as the poem progresses.

 Ideas for your own poems

 Step 1

As with Workshop 18, present the children with a series of questions to answer. Give them plenty of time and don't worry about spellings or presentation at this stage.

1. Where did you use to meet with friends to play out? Where do you meet them now?
- The park, the bus stop
- Someone's front gate, someone's house
- The steps outside the supermarket
- The wasteland, the woods
- The school yard
- Someone's back bedroom

My place was called the *Rec* (short for 'recreation ground').

2. Imagine that no one knows this place. What two things will help us picture it?
For example:
- The Rec had a sloping football pitch.
- There was a rope swing across the brook.
- An old lady's back fence panel was the perfect size for our goals.

3. When did you meet?
- Was it every night after school?
- Every Saturday?
- Late on summer evenings when it stayed light?

4. What did you do there? What games did you play?

- Tig, hide and seek
- Bike rides
- Making dens, rope swings
- Football
- Soldiers
- Sat and chatted
- Swapped toys or cards

5. Who did you meet? Which friends were always there?

Ask the class to write the names down the side of the page in a list. They can use real names or nicknames – whichever is best associated with them. For example:

- Ammo
- Mark
- Wigz
- Sutty

6. Can you think of *at least one* thing that you remember about each person?

- They knew the best jokes
- Always had chewing gum
- Never shared their sweets
- Laughed in a funny way
- Always wore the same shirt or trainers
- Always had messy hair
- Always had the best or most up-to-date clothes

So, you might have something like this:

- Ammo – had a tortoise called Flash
- Mark – had the full set of football stickers
- Wigz – good at football but would never pass or go in goal
- Sutty – did great impressions of the teachers

7. What memories stand out when you think of this place and these people?

These are usually funny things, like:

- The time Sutty fell off the rope swing into the water
- When Ammo's trousers split

Or it could be that they always did the same things there.

Step 2

Once you have all the ideas, you can use the principles and methods from the previous workshops to put the poem together.

Using repetition is an effective technique – it gives order and structure and something to hang the poem on. Try repeating the names, for example:

> We used to meet at the Rec
> Ammo, Mark, Wigz, Sutty and me
>
> Every Saturday afternoon
> Or late on summer evenings when it stayed light
> Ammo, Mark, Wigz, Sutty and me

> We'd play football on the sloping pitch
> Or rope swing across the muddy ditch
> On those Saturday afternoons
> Ammo, Mark, Wigz, Sutty and me
>
> Ammo – had a tortoise called Flash
> It was never that fast
> But it was painted like a superhero on the shell
>
> Mark – with his full set of football stickers
> Complete with wallet and swaps
> He even had the rare ones
>
> Wigz would never go in goal…
>
> I remember the time when…
>
> Those days at the Rec
> Ammo, Mark, Wigz, Sutty and me

Repeating other lines can be equally effective.

> I'll never forget those days
> Saturdays at the Rec
>
> We'd play football and cricket
> Jumpers for goalposts and old footballs
> Splintered cricket bats
> And wickets that were never the same size
> Swing on ropes across the muddy brook
> Or just go riding our bikes
> On those Saturdays at the Rec

Try focusing on one specific memory – start with this and then bring in other details:

> That time that Sutty split his trousers
> So funny
> We were playing football when…

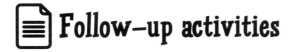

Follow-up activities

Remembering where
- Invite the children to write a poem based just on a description of the place itself.

Friends forever
- Challenge the class to write haiku about each of the friends who met there.

- Let them base the poem on how each friend got their nickname.

APPENDIX

 A few quick ideas

If you've read the workshops in this book then you'll have seen how a poem can grow quite quickly. Here are a few quick starting ideas that are based on some of the principles in the book.

1. Aww – I'm tell–ling

Say it out loud (as it's written) and you'll find the voice of the children quite easily.

Make a list of the things they 'tell of':

> Aww – I'm tell–ling
> He hit me
> She scribbled on my work
> He stuck his tongue out
> He took my pencil

Use the *Aww I'm tell-ling* line before each list item, exaggerating the rhythm and voice:

> Aww – I'm tell–ling
> He hit me
> Aww – I'm tell–ling
> She scribbled on my work
> Aww – I'm tell–ling
> He stuck his tongue out
> Aww – I'm tell–ling
> He took my pencil

Add a chorus, such as:

> I'm gonna tell my dad
> I'm gonna tell my mum
> I'm gonna tell my teacher
> I'm gonna get you done

Then divide into verse, chorus, verse, chorus.

2. Cannayavva

Write *Cannayavva* on the board. Say it out loud, making sure the children understand it's *Can I have a* (cannayavva reflects the way they say it).

Ask the children what sort of things they ask for when they are out shopping. For example:

> Cannayavva sweetie
> Cannayavva new toy
> Cannayavva football
> Cannayavaa nice cream

Then ask them what their parents say back. It could be something like:

> No you can't
> No you can't
> N – O – spells No!

This can be the chorus. You then have two different voices – the children in the verse and the parents in the chorus.

3. Doowhyaff2

Write this on the board and say it out loud. Explain that it's the same as *Do I have to* but it will sound better as one word in the poem.

Ask the children what sorts of things they have to do that they don't want to.

> Doowhyaff2 go to school?
> Doowhyaff2 eat my veg?
> Doowhyaff2 kiss my nan?
> Doowhyaff2 clean my teeth?

Say it out loud together and then work on a chorus. Ask what their parents say in response:

> Yes you do!
> Yes you do!
> Yes you do!
> Do – it – now!

Put it all together to create a poem with two voices.

4. Pirate chant

Pirates are always popular! Ask your class what you need to be a pirate and you'll build a list such as this:

- Hat
- Parrot
- Sword
- Beard
- Map
- Treasure

Using your best pirate voice, say each of them out loud for the class to repeat:

> Got my hat!
> Got my parrot!
> Got my sword!
> Got my beard!

Add a chorus:

> Yo ho ho
> Yo ho ho
> We are pirates
> Yo ho ho

5. It's not fair!

Ask the class to say *It's not fair*. You'll soon find the voice and tone for the poem.

Make a list together of things that are not fair:

- I can't play out
- We have to go to school
- He gets more than me
- It's my turn

Add the phrase *it's not fair*:

> It's not fair – I can't play out
> It's not fair – we have to go to school
> It's not fair – he gets more than me
> It's not fair – it's my turn

Edit some lines if necessary:

> It's not fair – he gets more

Add the usual type of chorus:

> It's not – it's not
> It's not fair
> It's not – it's not
> It's not fair

6. Mum for a day

If possible, read my poem 'Mum for a Day' from *Funny Poems* (pages 102–103). To create the humour in this poem, all I did was mix up the endings.

Along these lines, write a list of jobs mums and dads do:

- Mow the lawn
- Vacuum the carpet
- Cook the sausages
- Take the dog for a walk

Then change the endings and let the children decide which is funniest. You'll end up with lines like:

> Mow the carpet
> Vacuum the dog
> Cook the lawn
> Take the sausages for a walk

Add a beginning and an end. For the beginning, ask the children to explain why they are doing the housework:

> I'm grounded
> Mum said I had to do the housework and help at home
> But I got mixed up and
> [list of chores]

For the end, invite the class to consider what happened next. Were there any consequences?

7. Alphabets

If possible, read my poem 'An Alphabet of Alphabeastical Facts You Did Not Know You Knew' from *Silly Poems* (pages 42–43).

In this poem I just thought of animals for each letter and then strange, weird and wonderful things they couldn't do – the sillier the better. It doesn't have to rhyme so just have fun. For example:

> Aardvarks can't play tennis
> Bisons cannot tap dance
> Cows cannot ride motorbikes
> Dingos can't play didgeridoos

8. Tombstones and epitaphs

If possible, read the 'Terrible Tombstones' section from *Silly Poems* (pages 10–24).

These sorts of poems are short and fun. By their very nature they're very rarely more than four lines as they have to fit on a tombstone. It's mostly a case of thinking of funny ways to die. It will often follow this sort of structure:

> Here lies the body of [name]
> [Followed by the reason for their demise – often in rhyme]

For example:

> Here lies the body of Billy Brown
> Fell in the toilet – then he drowned

Or maybe write one about a teacher:

> Here lies the body
> Of sweet Miss B
> Died of boredom
> In literacy

9. Don't put Gran in goal

This is another cartoon-style poem. Together, think of reasons why Gran shouldn't go in goal:

> She's too slow
> She might fall asleep
> She'd rather have a cup of tea
> She might knit the nets
> Her false teeth might fall out
> And they'll burst the ball

Repeat the line every two to three lines:

> She's too slow
> She might fall asleep
> Don't put Gran in goal

> She'd rather have a cup of tea
> She might knit the nets
> Don't put Gran in goal

Think of other people and places where they shouldn't be:

> Don't let Dad cook dinner
> Don't let Mum go dancing
> Don't give Grandad an electric guitar

10. Mixed-up monsters

Write a list of animals or creatures on the board:
- Buffalo
- Crocodile
- Monkey
- Hippopotamus
- Rhinoceros
- Gorilla
- Shark
- Porcupine
- Anteater

Then mix up the animals, taking a beginning from one and the end of another. Try out various possibilities and choose the one that sounds best:
- Buffadile
- Buffarilla
- Buffapotamus
- Cronkey
- Rhinocerark
- Porcupilla

Then take aspects of both creatures to create a new creature:

> Porcupilla – spiny back
> Porcupilla – beats his chest

Ask questions to build up the rest of the poem. *Where does it live? What does it do? What does it look like?*

Poems to be performed

All poems sound better when read out loud and performed. Every poem in every book could benefit from this. I've chosen a few that I think you'll like and that have a wide range of performance styles, voices, and so on. You will find your own as well.

Animal Poems
'Chicken Dinner' by Valerie Bloom
'Don't Call Alligator Long-Mouth…' by John Agard
'H25' by Adrian Henri
'I Wannabe a Wallaby' by David Whitehead
'The Eagle' by Lord Tennyson
'The New Gnus' by John Foster
The Pied Piper of Hamelin by Robert Browning
'The Whale's Hymn' by Brian Patten

Dinosaur Poems
'Bored to Death' by Philip Waddell
'Dinosaur Discovery' by Andrew Collett
'Dinosaur Museum' by Peter Dixon
'Rex T's Wreckers Yard' by Paul Cookson
'The King of All the Dinosaurs' by Paul Cookson
'The Smellysaurus' by Henry Priestman and
    Les Glover
'What Colour?' by Colin West
'We Want Our Lovely Teachers Back' by David
    Harmer

Disgusting Poems
'A Disgusting Poem' by Fred Sedgwick
'Gran's Dog' by John Foster
'Head Lice' by Liz Brownlee
'Horrible' by Michael Rosen
'Our Dog' by John Kitching
'Pimple Potion Number Nine' by Mike Johnson
'The Day I Got My Finger…' by Brian Patten
'Unusual Taste' by Stewart Henderson

Family Poems
'A Step-Ladder' by Laurelle Rond
'Check the Board!' by Patricia Leighton
'Clickerty-Clackerty High-Heel Song' by Moira Clark
'Hot Potato' by Michael Rosen
'Kisses' by Ian Souter
'My Brother' by Michael Rosen
'My Family's Sleeping Late Today' by Jack Prelutsky
'My Hero' by Patricia Leighton

Funny Poems
'April Fool in School' by Ian Bland
'Baboons' Bottoms' by Coral Rumble
'Colonel Fazackerley' by Charles Causley
'Combinations' by Mary Ann Hoberman
'George Who Played with a Dangerous Toy…'
    by Hilaire Belloc
'Parent's Evening' by Roger Stevens
'School for Witches' by Gerard Benson
'Uncle Frank' by John Foster

Magic Poems
'Cherry Croak…' by Tony Mitton
'Dragonbirth' by Judith Nicholls
'Dragon Dance' by Max Fatchen
'Eeka Neeka' by Walter de la Mare
'Listen!' by Lilian Moore
'Merlin's Mynah' by Tony Mitton
'Mummy?' by David Poulter
'The Marvellous Trousers' by Richard Edwards

Pet Poems
'Barry's Budgie! Beware!' by David Harmer
'Four Crazy Pets' by Paul Cookson
'I Had a Little Cat' by Charles Causley
'My Dog, He Is an Ugly Dog' by Jack Prelutsky
'Pet Shop Rap' by Coral Rumble
'Poem Left Hopefully Lying Around Before Christmas'
    by Eric Finney
'Talking Turkeys!' by Benjamin Zephaniah
'War Dog' by Ian Souter

School Poems
'A Teacher's Lament' by Kalli Dakos
'Bully for You' by Ian Souter
'Colour of My Dreams' by Peter Dixon
'Conversation Piece' by Gareth Owen
'Infant Art' by Jennifer Curry
'Late' by Judith Nicholls
'Nativity Play' by Peter Dixon
'Schoolitis' by Brian Patten

Silly Poems
'Dog's Swear Words' by Roger Stevens
'Epitaph' by David Horner
'Epitaph for the Last Martian' by Paul Cookson
'Jumble Sale Offer' by Redvers Brandling
'Never Seen…' by Brian Moses
'Nonsense II' by Spike Milligan
'The Total Flop' by Nick Toczek
'Why You Should Never Play on Roads'
    by David Harmer

Spooky Poems
'Duppy Dan' by John Agard
'Hallowe'en' by Daphne Schiller
'I'd Rather Not Tell' by David Orme
'In the Castle of Gloom' by Wes Magee
'Quieter Than Snow' by Berlie Doherty
'The Haunted Poem' by Paul Cookson
'The Longest Journey in the World' by Michael Rosen
'Watch Your Teacher Carefully' by David Harmer

Model poems

Now you have looked at various ways of writing your own poems, here are a few poems that can be used as models for the children's poems. Copy them, adapt them, use them as starting points, rewrite them.

Animal Poems
'Earth-Worm' by Leonard Clark
'Elephantasia' by David Whitehead
'Patterning' by Coral Rumble
'Snail' by David Poulter
'The A–Z of Bopping Birds' by James Carter

Dinosaur Poems
'A Dinosaur ABC' by Marian Swinger
'Here Come the Dinosaurs' by Rita Ray
'Rhymes From the Dinosaur Nursery' by David
    Horner
'Terrible Lizards – One to Ten' by Celia Gentles

Disgusting Poems
'Advice To Anyone Cooped up in a Hot Car on a
    Long Journey' by John Irving Clarke
'Gran's Big Bloomers' by Clare Bevan
'Message on the Table' by David Kitchen
'Ten Things to Do with a Dead Hamster'
    by Tony Bradman
'Underneath Dad's Armchair' by Andrew Collett

Family Poems
'Face Pulling Contests' by Brian Moses
'For Sale' by Patricia Leighton
'Questions' by Trevor Harvey
'Recipe for a Disastrous Family Picnic' by Ian
    Souter

Funny Poems
'Three Frazzles in a Frimple' by Brian Patten
'Three Silly Things to Do with a Sock' by Jan Dean
'Trying To Hide the Really Rude SNOG Words'
    by David Harmer

Magic Poems
'A Very Old Spell to Say Out Loud to Get Rid of
    Warts' translated by Michael Rosen
'Jack's Magic Wand' by David Harmer
'Lion' by Celia Warren
'The Woman of Water' by Adrian Mitchell

Pet Poems
'My Fish Can Ride a Bicycle' by Jack Prelutsky
'Teacher's Pet' by Tony Mitton
'The Great Gerbil Hunt' by Judith Nicholls
'Who Am I?' by John Kitching

School Poems
'At the End of School Assembly' by Simon Pitt
'Ten School Computers' by Charles Thomson
'The Classroom Circle of Friends' by Wes Magee
'Do You Know My Teacher?' by John Rice
'Recipe for a Class Outing' by Sue Cowling

Silly Poems
'Riddle Me Wrong' by David Harmer
'Ten Rhyming Things That Should Not Be Eaten'
    by John Coldwell
'A Batty Booklist' by John Foster
'Frack To Bont' by Paul Cookson

Spooky Poems
'The Haunted Poem' by Paul Cookson
'Gobbledespook' by Gina Douthwaite
'I'd Rather Not Tell' by David Orme
'Green Man' by Anon

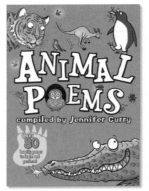
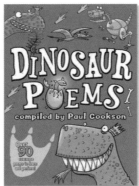

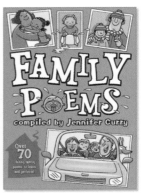
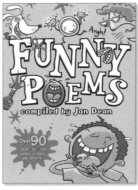
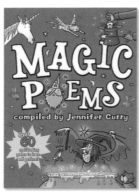
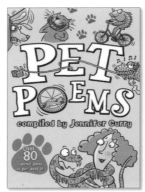
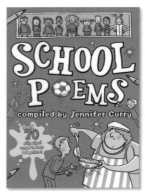
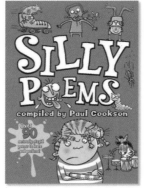
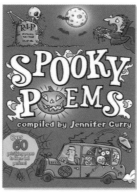